The Prog Rock Trivia Book

Just a Collection of Answers to Curious Questions About All Things Progressive Rock

Written by
Gian-Luca Di Rocco

© Gian-Luca Di Rocco 2022
ISBN: 9798427904490

Table of Contents

Proclamation 1

Prologue 3

SIDE ONE:
Answers? **Questions!** 11

   Chapter One — The Artists 13

      Part A — British Progressive Rock 13

      Part B — The Canterbury Scene 17

      Part C — Italian Progressive Rock 18

      Part D — German Progressive Rock 19

      Part E — North American Progressive Rock 20

      Part F — Progressive Rock from the Rest of Europe ... 21

      Part G — Prog from the Rest of the World 23

   Chapter Two — The Albums 25

   Chapter Three — The Tracks 33

   Chapter Four — The Lyrics 39

   Chapter Five — The Concerts 43

   Chapter Six — Plaudits and Pundits 47

   Chapter Seven — Progressive Rock at the Cinema 51

   Chapter Eight — Progressive Rock on Television 57

   Chapter Nine — Prog Rock Quotes 63

   Chapter Ten — Miscellaneous 69

Table of Contents

SIDE TWO:
Questions? **Answers!** 73

- Chapter Eleven — The Artists 75
  - Part A — British Progressive Rock 75
  - Part B — The Canterbury Scene 78
  - Part C — Italian Progressive Rock.. 79
  - Part D — German Progressive Rock..80
  - Part E — North American Progressive Rock 81
  - Part F — Progressive Rock From the Rest of Europe.................. 82
  - Part G — Prog From the Rest of the World 83
- Chapter Twelve — The Albums 85
- Chapter Thirteen — The Tracks 95
- Chapter Fourteen — The Lyrics..101
- Chapter Fifteen — The Concerts 105
- Chapter Sixteen — Plaudits and Pundits 109
- Chapter Seventeen — Progressive Rock at the Cinema 113
- Chapter Eighteen — Progressive Rock on Television 119
- Chapter Nineteen — Quotes 123
- Chapter Twenty — Miscellaneous 129

Bibliography 135
About the Author 137

Proclamation

I hereby dedicate this book to all the progressive rock artists that have entertained me over the years through both recorded music and live performances I've been fortunate enough to attend. I'd also like to thank my partner Heather Murray for once again helping out with the editing, the layout of the book and the cover design, and also for having pretty cool taste in music — which goes against the stereotype that women don't like progressive rock.

Proclamation

Prologue

So why write a trivia book focusing on progressive rock?

The main reason is that, until now, there hasn't been one — which seemed a strange omission in the marketplace, given the popularity of the genre. However, this is perhaps typical of this particular musical style, which tends to be marginalized or under-represented in various forms of media or through critical appreciation.

Progressive rock — also known popularly as "Prog Rock" or simply "Prog" — no longer seems to be as consistently and harshly condemned or as scathingly criticized as it was by much of the first generation of music critics who wrote in the 1970s and 80s, but the influence of the media continues. Many in the media nowadays don't mention if a certain band (even if extremely well known such as *Pink Floyd*) is considered a progressive rock band.

At the time of writing, some of the most commercially successful and influential rock bands of all time still not inducted into the American so-called "Rock and Roll Hall of Fame" are Prog bands (e.g., *Jethro Tull, Emerson Lake & Palmer, Mike Oldfield, Alan Parsons*, and the extraordinarily influential *King Crimson*), due in large part to the inductees being chosen on the personal whim of a handful of individuals, one of whom has included notorious "anti-progressive rock" critic Dave Marsh.

There is still a school of thought that progressive rock was "killed" by punk rock in the late 1970s, which is not only untrue globally, but a dubious claim even in the one nation where punk did become hugely commercially successful as a musical style and fad: the UK (some of the questions in this book will be, in their own way, examining the veracity of these claims). Music documentaries, particularly those about rock music in general, will often downplay the importance or continued success of Prog.

All these factors contribute to people not realizing how popular and successful the genre truly has been and continues to be. In fact, it is still not that uncommon for me to field questions such as "What do you mean by *progressive rock?*" or "Who counts as a *progressive rock* band?" when people learn that I predominately listen to progressive rock. I am hoping this little book will do its own extremely tiny part in helping to change that, and to raise awareness for the genre.

My own journey of discovering this music may provide a good example of the marginalization of the genre, or at least the term "progressive rock."

I had been listening to and collecting the music of several progressive rock bands for a few years before I became aware that they were all generally considered "progressive rock" artists. In the beginning, I wasn't listening to *Jethro Tull, Yes, The Moody Blues, King Crimson, ELP, Pink Floyd,* and *Genesis* and deliberately seeking out and hearing more of the genre *because* they were all progressive rock bands — on the contrary, I heard these bands when they were played by the local "classic rock" radio station that I was listening to in my teens and, despite the fact that none of these bands sounded like each other, they were the ones that appealed to me the most from the station's broadcasts. It was only in my early 20s, after a few years of exploring these bands, that a friend of mine listed the bands that I liked to his older brother — a Prog fan himself — who then uttered the term "progressive rock," which was the first time I was exposed to the phrase. Notably, this exposure to the term **did not** come through it being used in the media.

Where progressive rock has perhaps not helped itself in preventing its marginalization by the media, and one of the most challenging aspects to deal with in any book about progressive rock, is that what actually constitutes Prog is a debate that has emerged since the genre was created — and will probably never be definitively answered. Even Bill Martin's academic work on the topic of progressive rock (*Listening to the Future: The Time of Progressive Rock* — one of the earliest books exclusively dedicated to discussing progressive rock and seeking to define it as a genre) claims that the aforementioned *Pink Floyd* doesn't count as "Prog," and provides a rationale for why that is the case (largely based around the fact that the most of the band members were not virtuoso musicians). Now, I haven't seen any other publications or journalism which agreed with this assertion, but that this argument is put forward in such a definitive tome speaks volumes about the debate of "what counts."

(That this book, published in 1998 — three decades after the genre was created in the late 1960s — was only the 4th book published that was focused on discussing the Prog Rock genre as a whole (with the first serious musicological work, and the 2nd book overall, having been published just one year earlier) also speaks to how unrepresented in the media progressive rock was for decades.)

All of the (many) books I have collected on progressive rock acknowledge that there is some debate as to what artists and musical output constitute the genre. Some of the books are more inclusive than others; I tend to be on the inclusive side.

I will not be offering my own definition *per se*. I am, above all, primarily a fan of the music and, I feel, one who understands intuitively from over three decades of listening to the genre what "counts" or sounds "progressive," aided and abetted by books such as Edward Macan's *Rocking the Classics — English Progressive Rock and the Counterculture* in putting the genre into a proper framework and context. I am not, however, a musician (you won't find, for example, any questions on "Which progressive rock track is in 25/8 time?" or "What is the 574th note that can be heard in *Thick as a Brick*?"). Suffice it to say that each musical artist included in a question in this book has, apart from my own feelings, opinions, and thoughts as a fan and listener, generally been considered (or at the very least, considered by more than one reputable, published source) to be a progressive rock artist or at the very least part of the broader Prog family.

For anyone who is reading this book and becomes outraged that one of the answers to a question turns out to be regarding an artist that they don't personally consider to be a "progressive rock" artist, my apologies in advance — however, that's part and parcel of this genre, which has always been about breaking musical boundaries and combining different musical genres with rock music to see where it could go and what could be created from it.

The genre itself is, in my view, the most singularly inclusive musical genre in existence, incorporating a plethora of musical styles and an unlimited variety of different musical instruments into a rock context. This diversity is a large part of the appeal for a fan of the genre as a whole (e.g., if I want to listen to a bit of reggae, disco, or opera, I can do so by putting on various progressive rock albums in my collection which have tunes that incorporate those wildly varying styles), but it also means that the boundaries of the genre itself (and who is considered to be an artist within it) are somewhat blurred. As mentioned though, I am not just going by my own opinions and the instincts of an aficionado of this genre on what I believe "counts," but also considering what independent published sources recognize as progressive rock. A full bibliography can be found at the end of this book, in case the reader is curious regarding these sources.

Another thing I am *not* doing is defining Prog by only including those artists who consider themselves to be progressive rock artists, since that would probably eliminate 70% of the questions I could ask in this book — another bizarre trait of this genre is how many of the artists which have helped to define and create the genre have *denied being a part of it* or don't accept that the term applies to them.

A few other explanatory notes may be of assistance:

I have attempted to write a book that will appeal to the broadest possible audience — both the casual music listener and fan who might only have heard of the "big" bands in this genre, as well as the progressive rock aficionados and experts such as myself. This is a tricky balance, which I hope I have achieved, but this means I haven't included many questions on the more "obscure" artists in my collection of which I am a fan, particularly those "newer" bands who formed after the classic period and are performing and releasing new material to this day. My apologies to those artists and bands — the likes of *Phideaux, Beardfish, Pure Reason Revolution, Pineapple Thief, Eris Pluvia*, and so many more that I could mention. However, I just felt that book which was filled with

Prologue

questions on *Wobbler* (a fantastic band from Norway that I recommend every progressive rock fan should check out if they have not already done so — start with the album **From the Silence to Somewhere**) would be a challenge to make of interest to a broader market.

Newer progressive rock artists are included, but they tend to be the ones that have achieved a reasonable amount of commercial or mainstream success (a few of them are listed on the back cover of the book). As such, my approach has been to focus on the most famous progressive rock bands, mainly from the classic period of the late 60s and 70s, although the notably successful bands from the 80s onwards are also substantially featured. This will not just be the incredibly commercially-successful bands like *Pink Floyd, Jethro Tull, Yes, Rush, The Moody Blues*, etc., but the artists that tended to at least enjoy chart success of some kind or a large and consistent cult following over the years. Not just featuring British bands, but successful bands at either a mainstream or cult level from across the world.

What makes this challenging, of course, is that the more famous a band, the more difficult it is to find something trivial about them that would be worth including as a question. There are no questions in this book such as "Who was the bass player for *Pink Floyd*?" that only someone barely familiar with the band would find challenging — instead, I have tried to find questions for which the answers will (hopefully) be considered interesting in their own right, regardless of how intimately familiar with a particular band or artist the reader might be.

I have also tried to avoid questions for which the answers seem to be now too-well known (e.g., I didn't bother to ask "Which progressive rock artist did Sid Vicious indicate he was a fan of when interviewed about his musical influences and heroes on BBC Radio in 1977?" because the story of the *Sex Pistols* frontman taking a Peter Hammill solo album with him to that interview has been repeated so many times now in so many different publications that it no longer seemed trivial enough to bother to ask people about). On the other hand, I *was* tempted to include a question on "Which *Van Der Graaf Generator* album cover can be seen emblazoned upon the t-shirt that *Doctor Who* actor Matthew Waterhouse is wearing in the Blu-ray extra documentary on the making of Tom Baker's final story

Prologue

Logopolis?" but the answer seemed *too* trivial, because it's doubtful how many people reading this book (other than *Doctor Who* fans or perhaps some *Van Der Graaf Generator* fans) would even care. (The answer, incidentally, is their 2011 album, **A Grounding in Numbers** and, despite its super-triviality, I still think the info is cool, so I had to slip it into this book somewhere).

As such, I have tried to strive for a happy medium, but I suppose whether I have succeeded is, as *The Moody Blues* might say, a question of balance.

I've also tried to avoid asking questions where the answer can easily be looked up on Wikipedia (e.g., "When was *Happy the Man*'s 3rd album, recorded in 1979, finally released?" — it would be easy enough to go online and see that the answer is 1990). Inevitably, many of the questions here could be "verified" on Wikipedia (scare quotes used because the site has been known to include errors by the volunteers who contribute or edit it as a resource), but do yourself a favour and don't turn to the internet to look up any of the answers first, instead of trying to answer the question. I'm confident that you'll enjoy this book much more if you avoid taking that step and read the book in the spirit in which it was intended.

Another thing to note is that fans of progressive *metal* may be disappointed, as there are not that many questions related to that particular sub-genre of progressive rock (some may argue it's a "sister genre" rather than a sub-genre, but let's not get into that here). The main reason being that, other than *Opeth* and *Ayreon* (of which there are some questions related to), I'm not particularly a huge fan of that genre (and with the former, I am more familiar with their out and out progressive rock albums rather than their earlier period as a Death Metal band). For the most part, I wanted to write about bands that I am not just a fan of, but also have acquired a wealth of knowledge about (be it through having listened to their albums which I have purchased and poured over the liner notes of countless times over the decades, or having read further about as I thirsted for more knowledge about them). As such, other than a handful of questions related to the two bands mentioned above (and

Dream Theater), there is a relative dearth of questions related to this particular genre.

In any event, I sincerely hope that there will be much in this book for the novice and the expert alike to enjoy. If nothing else, I hope that this book helps to raise more awareness for some of the more quirky, eccentric, and interesting rock music artists out there — and, of course, the progressive music they have made, which has brought an incalculable amount of musical pleasure to my own ears for decades.

Prologue

SIDE ONE:
Answers?
Questions!

Chapter One — The Artists

Part A — British Progressive Rock

1. What famous keyboardist recommended drummer Ian Wallace to Robert Fripp as a potential new member of *King Crimson*, which led to his joining the band for the "Islands" album in 1971?

2. Garth Watt Roy of the band *The Greatest Show on Earth* had previously featured in which progressive blues-rock band that was named after a bird?

3. Tony Iommi pretended to play guitar for which legendary progressive rock band in a famous performance which originally went unreleased for decades?

4. Who was the first British act to be signed to A&M Records?

5. Who was *Jethro Tull*'s drummer for their performance at the 1982 Prince's Trust Rock Gala?

6. *Roxy Music* lead singer Bryan Ferry had earlier failed an audition as a replacement lead singer for which seminal progressive rock band?

7. Which progressive rock band did Elton John fail an audition for in 1970?

8. After Roger Hodgson left *Supertramp*, which progressive rock guitarist did the band get to replace him by playing on the band's

Chapter One — The Artists · Answers? Questions!

16-minute epic title track for the album **Brother Where You Bound**?

9. Who burned an American flag on stage at the Royal Albert Hall in 1968, resulting in his group being banned from ever playing there again?

10. Which progressive rock band won the 1974 Melody Maker Battle of the Bands competition?

11. Who did the press dub the "van Gogh of the Saxophone"?

12. Which progressive rock band did John Lennon praise in a radio interview he gave in New York in 1973?

13. In between his stint as a founding member of *Renaissance* and joining *The Strawbs*, keyboardist John Hawken worked in what non-musical capacity?

14. What later-famous band was the lyricist for the *King Crimson* album **Larks Tongues in Aspic** in, *before* he wrote the lyrics for that album?

15. Who played saxophone on *The Rolling Stones* hit "Miss You"?

16. Who played saxophone on *Pink Floyd*'s album **A Momentary Lapse of Reason**?

17. How old was Andy Ward when he joined *The Brew*, the band that two years later would be re-named (and play their first gig as) *Camel*?

18. Bassist Rick Kemp of progressive folk-rocker *Steeleye Span* was also a member of what progressive rock band for a grand total of three days before leaving, whilst declaring that the demands placed upon him by the band leader were impossible to meet?

19. What profession did keyboard player Stephen Houston take up after he left the band *Fruupp*?

20. When Patrick Moraz successfully auditioned to replace Rick Wakeman in *Yes*, with whose keyboards did he perform the audition?

21. Who once responded to a fan letter complaining that he could only see the lead guitarist for 45% of the show with a letter that refunded 55% of the ticket price along with an instruction to never see the band perform live again?

22. Who once responded to a critic who criticized a track on the album for being a lousy song by indicating that the track in question "had no singing on it, and therefore, is not a song"?

23. According to the manager of the band he was in, what individual would "ring up in a complete state, telling me he's Christ and pinned to a wall. I'd have to spend hours talking him down..."?

24. Who was presented as the fifth member of *The Moody Blues* in their lavish comeback press launch held in the UK in 1978 in place of Mike Pinder, who had not flown over from the US for the event?

25. Who reportedly once referred to himself as a "poor man's Peter Hammill"?

26. Which band reformed after a live 19-minute version of one of their classic epic progressive rock tracks was played on the radio on the BBC's Friday Rock Show in 1982?

27. Which band wrote their tracks by having the guitarist mail his sheet music to a poet living in Cornwall, who would then write lyrics to them and mail them back to the guitarist?

28. What did the acronym of the short-lived band *XYZ* — featuring Jimmy Page, Chris Squire, and Alan White — stand for?

29. Which pioneering progressive rock artist started off life in the then-fledgling computer business as a computer programmer?

30. Which bass player stated that the band he was in didn't see itself as part of the progressive rock movement in 1969 because it was "singles-oriented in 1969 and we were an album band"?

31. The members of the obscure band *Sisyphus* would go on to comprise the 4/5ths of the original line-up of what much more famous progressive rock band?

32. In between the break-up of *Van Der Graaf Generator* at the end of 1976 and being called back into the band for two live shows that would be recorded as the live LP **Vital** in 1978 as *Van Der Graaf*, what occupation did David Jackson have?

33. Which British progressive rock band had the distinction of having their music played by all four BBC radio stations in the same week in 1973, despite the fact that the radio stations were playing different styles of music which catered to different audiences?

34. Which British progressive rock band had the distinction of having all 18 members of its band and entourage arrested in the state of Indiana in September 1974?

35. The entire canteen staff of a roadhouse diner named *The Blue Boar* once adoringly surrounded the members of *The Strawbs* when they arrived at the canteen — having mistaken them for what other progressive rock band?

36. The four members of the band *10cc* had previously played together with what progressive rock outfit?

37. Who was Kimberley Barrington Frost better known as?

38. Elton John reportedly pitched his songs "Your Song" and "Skyline Pigeon" to be used by the members of which progressive rock band?

39. Which progressive rock singer was, as a youth, once thrown out of a school choir for singing too loudly?

40. Which British progressive rock band topped the "Billboard FM Action" charts, according to an advertisement on the November 23rd, 1974 issue of *Billboard*?

Part B — The Canterbury Scene

41. The names Simeon Sasparella (guitarist), Basil Dowling (drummer), Njerogi Gategaka (bass) and Sam Lee-Uff (organist) were the pseudonyms for which four progressive rock artists in order to avoid potential contractual difficulties with the record company they were signed to under their real names?

42. Which member of *Gong* claimed to have first met the founders of the band (Daevid Allen and Gilly Smith) whilst he was living in a cave?

43. On which 1975 Canterbury scene progressive rock release does Elton John appear as a session musician for two tracks?

44. Who phoned writer William Burroughs to obtain permission to use *The Soft Machine* as the name for their band?

45. For which three bands did *Caravan* act as a supporting artist in their Australian tour of January 1973?

46. Which Canterbury scene musician was once described in an issue of *Melody Maker* from the 1970s as "one of the few rock singers who can actually sing"?

47. The father of Damon Albarn (of the Britpop band *Blur)* co-managed which Canterbury Prog band circa 1969?

48. Robert Wyatt became paralyzed from the waist down after falling from a fourth-floor window during a birthday party for which Canterbury artist?

49. Whose first name(s) are actually Julian Frederick Gordon?

50. Which bass player from the Canterbury scene was born in Egypt and grew up in Kenya?

51. Which member of the Canterbury scene was born in Fiji?

52. Which Canterbury scene artist had a number 1 album on the Belgian album charts the week of October 12th, 1974?

53. Although he never recorded with the band, who was *Gong's* violin player circa 1971?

Part C — Italian Progressive Rock

54. Which Italian band's last release of the 1970s included a song that, when translated into English, is called "Ice Cream Cone"?

55. Who wrote the lyrics for *Le Orme*'s English-language release of **Felona e Serona**?

56. Who was the first Italian rock band to have an album chart on the US Top 200 Billboard charts?

57. Which Italian progressive rock band had a single that rode the top of the Italian Hit Parade (aka the Italian Singles chart) for six weeks in 1972?

58. What Italian progressive rock album do Ian Anderson and Steve Hackett both play on?

59. Which Italian progressive rock band had some of their key members previously playing in a band called *Sally Duck*?

60. Which instrumental track by *Goblin* hit number one on the Italian Hit Parade charts for five weeks?

61. Which Italian band claims to have, in the same album, both the longest *and* shortest tracks in the history of Italian Prog?

62. Which Italian band released what they considered to be the "first Italian rock opera," and what was the album in question?

63. What Italian beat band released a progressive rock concept album concerning a murder committed by the mafia?

64. Which Italian band released a concept album sequel to **Felona e Sorona** by *Le Orme*?

Answers? Questions!   Chapter One — The Artists

Part D — German Progressive Rock

65. Which progressive rock artist is the track "We All Thought We Knew You" by *Birth Control* written about?

66. What German progressive rock band played featured members who went by such stage names as "Toni Moff Mollo," "Mist," "Lupo," "Tarzan," and "Willi Wildschwein"?

67. According to the liner notes of the CD re-release of one of their albums, which German progressive band was the first German rock band of any kind to get an album in the American Top 40 Billboard charts, and with what album?

68. The members of *Marillion* attended a concert at the Marquee Club in 1984 that was given as part of a "farewell" tour in the UK by which German Prog rock band?

69. Which band's last album apparently (according to the liner notes of their official CD re-releases of their albums) translates roughly as "We don't give a shit what happens after we're gone"?

70. Which German Prog band had the entirety of a double album broadcast national on German radio, helping it to go Gold in its native country?

71. Which German progressive band was named after a *Deep Purple* track?

72. Which German band managed to get a Top 10 album on the UK charts in 1975?

73. Which German progressive band has been credited as having released the first-ever German Rock Opera?

74. Which German band performed live at the 1972 Olympic Games in Munich?

Part E — North American Progressive Rock

75. *Klaatu*'s final studio album, **Magentalane**, was recorded in which town north of Toronto?

76. What band did *Arc Angel* ultimately become?

77. By what name was Gary Weinrib better known?

78. Prior to joining *Styx* as Dennis DeYoung's replacement on keyboards and vocals, Lawrence Gowan (aka Gowan) had a successful solo career in Canada, including the hit single "Moonlight Desires" featuring which famous progressive rock singer not only as a second vocalist but also in the official music video?

79. Which American band released their own cover of "Fanfare for the Common Man" five years before *Emerson, Lake and Palmer* released theirs?

80. Which American band was originally signed by the same guy who had created *The Monkees*?

81. Under what name was James Jeffrey Plewman better known professionally?

82. In which respective countries did Canadian band *Saga* have their earliest hit single and greatest longevity of success?

83. Who turned down an offer from David Gilmour to play guitar on one of his solo albums?

84. According to Dennis De Young, who came backstage to a *Styx* concert and told him that his own band was hugely influenced by *Styx*'s **The Serpent is Rising** LP?

85. With which St. Catharines band did Neil Peart play, prior to joining *Rush*?

86. Which 1982 US Top 40 hit by a solo artist did *Saga* drummer Steve Negus play on?

Part F — Progressive Rock from the Rest of Europe

87. Luxembourg's *No Name* dedicated the track "Horizon" to which British progressive rock band?

88. Which French progressive rock band included a member who would go on to co-produce and write most of the songs of the most successful French-language music album of all time?

89. According to Daevid Allen, the drummer of which band would hit the members of his band with a stick onstage if they played a note incorrectly?

90. The Finnish band *Wigwam* recorded what song after they played a free concert in Hyde Park in London on August 30th, 1975?

91. What band, operating under an earlier name than the one they later became famous for as a Prog band, heiped to open the 1972 Olympics in Munich alongside *The Mahavishnu Orchestra*?

92. With what major 70s French Prog band did John Wetton record a few tracks?

93. Which Swedish progressive rock artist had one of his songs covered by Jimi Hendrix?

94. After leaving *King Crimson*, violinist David Cross played on which French progressive rock album?

95. Which progressive rock band from continental Europe managed to score ten Top 10 singles in their homeland from 1970 to 1979?

96. Which Yugoslavian progressive rock band from the 1970s took their name from a Hermann Hesse book?

97. By 1977, not including albums by *Ange*, which French progressive rock band had the highest-selling album by a French rock band?

98. Which Norwegian progressive rock band ended up changing their name midway through their career, when they became aware of another band from Germany already had the same name?

99. Which French progressive rock vocalist provided uncredited lead and backing vocals to fellow French Prog rockers *Mona Lisa* for their January 1977 album **Le petit violon de mr. grégoire?**

100. Which Swedish progressive band managed to score a #1 album on the German charts in the 2010s?

101. Who broke both his heels while rehearsing a stunt for a concert, causing his band's late-1974 tour to be cancelled?

102. Which progressive rock band managed the unusual feat of having two different singles simultaneously make the UK Top 20 in January 1973, without either track featuring any lyrics?

103. Which famous progressive rock artist's grandfather was apparently assassinated, with bullets hitting his body in the sign of a cross?

104. Which progressive rock band from continental Europe has the unique distinction of having a song make the finals of the famous (or infamous, depending on one's point of view) Eurovision Song Contest back in the 1970s?

Part G — Prog from the Rest of the World

105. German electronic artist Klaus Schulze produced two albums by which Japanese progressive rock band?

106. Péter Pejtsik of the Hungarian band *After Crying* guest-starred on the comeback album of which legendary South American band?

107. Which Australian progressive rock band's debut album made it to #12 on the Australian album charts?

108. Which Caribbean-born progressive rock artist released two concept albums based on a trilogy of successful science fiction novels he authored and published in the 1970s?

109. Which South American progressive rock band in 1974 released a concept album that included a song about every major traditional and influential institution in that particular country?

110. The Argentinian progressive rock band *Aquelarre* was formed by an ex-member of which legendary Argentinian band that had been widely dubbed the "Argentinian Beatles"?

Chapter Two — The Albums

1. Who is the only member of *Genesis* circa 1975 to 1977 who did not play on the 1975 LP **Voyage of the Acolyte**?

2. Who produced the Daryl Hall (of Hall & Oates) album **Sacred Songs**?

3. With over 17 million sales, which album is considered the biggest-selling instrumental album of all time?

4. **In the Wake of Poseidon** was the highest-charting *King Crimson* album in the UK, hitting #4 in 1970 — what were the three albums charting higher that same week?

5. Which progressive rock drummer co-produced a Steve Hillage solo album in the late 1970s?

6. How many weeks in a row did **Tubular Bells** by Mike Oldfield initially stay on the UK album charts?

7. Which progressive rock album released in 1972 provided the name for one of the first bands formed by *The Mars Volta* vocalist Cedric Bixler-Zavala?

8. Which progressive rock album title from 1973 was referenced in the lyrics to a track which appeared on an album that reached #1 in the charts in 1985 in the UK?

9. What was the highest-charting album in the US for *Gentle Giant*, and in which country was this chart performance bettered?

Chapter Two — The Albums   Answers? Questions!

10. Released in 1975, in what year did *Camel*'s **The Snow Goose** go Silver in the UK?

11. By what name was *Caravan*'s **Cunning Stunts** album originally slated to be released under, only to be renamed after another band released an LP bearing the same name slightly ahead of them?

12. During the two weeks that *The Moody Blues* **Seventh Sojourn** hit #1 in the Canadian album charts in 1973, what album sat at #2 each week?

13. Recordings for the *PFM* album **Live in the USA** (which was released under the title **Cook** for the US market) were taken from live concerts held in which two countries?

14. Which progressive rock album stayed at the top of the Italian charts for 12 weeks in 1972?

15. Which album by a German progressive rock band sold 200,000 copies the year of its release — apparently reaching higher in the German charts than the most recent albums released by *Genesis* and *Queen* that year?

16. Which progressive rock album did Pete Townsend of *The Who* call "An Uncanny Masterpiece"?

17. At what position did *Fruupp*'s debut album first enter the UK charts?

18. What was the name of the whale character, who is the subject of the 1979 concept album **Flossengel** by *Novalis*?

19. Which album by *Machiavel* enabled them to become the first Belgium group of any kind to have a record sell more than 50,000 copies?

20. The week of October 26th, 1974, there were as many as 17 progressive rock albums in the US Billboard Top 200 (18, if you count *10cc*'s **Sheet Music** LP) — in alphabetical order, the artists included *Electric Light Orchestra; Emerson, Lake and Palmer; Focus; Genesis; Gentle Giant; Hawkwind; Jethro Tull; Nektar; Mike Oldfield; Renaissance; Rush; Traffic; Triumvirat; Rick*

Answers? Questions!   Chapter Two — The Albums

Wakeman; and *Frank Zappa.* Of these 15 artists (*ELP* and *Zappa* had two albums each, for a total of 17), which band had the earliest recorded material in the charts that week?

21. What progressive rock album gives a credit on its vinyl sleeve to a Judo Consultant?

22. Ian Anderson has often claimed that **The Broadsword and the Beast** did not perform that well in the US but was the band's biggest selling album in Germany (where it hit #14 in comparison to hitting #19 in the US) — in what country did the album reach its highest chart position?

23. Who calls the **Union** album by *Yes* "Onion," and why?

24. The highest-charting *Renaissance* album in the UK was **A Song for All Seasons** at #35. In the US, it was **Novella** at #46. What was their highest charting album in Canada, according to RPM Weekly charts?

25. Which two progressive rock albums are among the top six albums for most weeks ever spent on the German album charts?

26. For the week of December 16th, 1972, which four progressive rock albums occupied spots in the Top 10 album charts in Canada?

27. What was the most commercially-successful album by German progressive rock band *Novalis*?

28. Which progressive rock band caused *The Beatles* to change the originally-planned name of their 1968 double-LP to simply **The Beatles** (more commonly known as "The White Album"), due to their earlier release of an identically-named album?

29. What album knocked Mike Oldfield's **Hergest Ridge** off the top of the UK album charts in 1974?

30. On what progressive rock album cover art can tiny models of *The Village People* be found?

31. The week of August 18th, 1973 might have been the proggiest week in Canadian music history, with the top three chart positions taken by *Deep Purple* (**Machine Head**) at #1, *Pink Floyd* at #2

Chapter Two — The Albums   Answers? Questions!

(**Dark Side of the Moon**), and *Jethro Tull* at #3 (**A Passion Play**). However, perhaps most interesting is that, simultaneously, a continental European Progressive rock band had three of its own albums in Canadian Top 100. What band was this, and what were the three albums?

32. Chart-position-wise, what was the most successful Steve Hillage album in the UK?

33. On which progressive rock album is Alan Parsons thanked for providing food?

34. What progressive rock album was the 6th best-selling album in Holland in 1979?

35. Which German progressive rock album's recording was significantly delayed by the band's vocalist and keyboard player obsessively playing chess every day in the recording studio?

36. Which 1970s progressive rock artist persuaded and encouraged Ian Anderson in the early 2010s to come up with a sequel album to *Jethro Tull*'s **Thick as a Brick**?

37. What band released a live album taken from concert performances from the famous Marquee Club, which had a title parodying a James Bond film?

38. What do the cover art for albums **Üdü Wüdü** by *Magma* and **Tales from the Lush Attic** by *IQ* have in common?

39. The lyrics to which album by an Italian progressive rock band were inspired by a mysterious 18th century Scottish musician, who loved the music of J.S. Bach so much that he believed himself to be the composer's natural son?

40. A guitar which once belonged to Pete Townsend of *The Who* was used by the guitarist of what French progressive rock band, for the recording of what album?

41. Which two albums, from two different progressive rock bands, hit #1 on the charts in Germany, each on two separate occasions (rather than in consecutive weeks) in 1982?

28

Answers? Questions! Chapter Two — The Albums

42. Which progressive rock album was originally released in the 1970s with a transparent vinyl disc and a transparent album sleeve?

43. Which progressive rock album reached #1 on the Italian album charts in 1972 and stayed there for six weeks, as part of a 35-week run in the Top 8 of the charts?

44. What album made this band the third-highest-selling German artist of 1976, behind only Udo Lindenberg and *Kraftwerk*?

45. Which classic progressive rock album from the 1970s was named after a café located on Portobello Road in London, England?

46. Which Italian progressive rock album had its cover art displayed for some time at the Museum of Modern Art in New York?

47. Which progressive rock band sold one of their albums by providing each buyer with a deed to one square foot of land in Wales?

48. *Saga* vocalist and keyboardist Michael Sadler decided he wanted to make progressive rock music after hearing side one of which British progressive rock album?

49. Which progressive concept album is about a person who travels back in time after taking some, well, time-travelling drugs?

50. Which band were the members of *The Alan Parsons Project* worried might do a concept album based on the works of Edgar Allen Poe before they did so with **Tales of Mystery and Imagination**?

51. Which solo album, put out by a member of *Yes*, featured two members of *Gryphon* as players?

52. What were the only two *Caravan* albums to crack the charts in the UK?

53. After having written about 99.5% of *Jethro Tull*'s songs on his own, when Ian Anderson finally released a solo album in 1983, what percentage of the tracks were written solely by him?

Chapter Two — The Albums   Answers? Questions!

54. In the progressive rock "hotbed" of Portugal, which three progressive rock-related albums made up 30% of the Top 10 of the Portuguese album charts the week of October 21st, 1978?

55. What do the solo albums **Olias of Sunhillow** by Jon Anderson and **Arc of a Diver** by Steve Winwood have in common?

56. At the time of writing (March 2022), what was the last Frank Zappa album to chart in the Canadian album charts?

57. Florian is the name of the main protagonist of what progressive rock concept album?

58. According to the November 29th, 1975 edition of *Cashbox*, what album was #5 on the Album Charts for Japan?

59. **Citadel** by *Starcastle* managed to reach what chart position on the US Billboard charts?

60. *Uriah Heep* managed to crack the Top 10 of which Eastern European nation's Album charts the week of May 11th, 1974 with **Sweet Deceiver**?

61. Which progressive rock album made it into the Top 10 album charts for Denmark for the week of September 14th, 1974?

62. What percentage of the Top 15 selling albums in Belgium for the week of October 12th, 1974 can be reasonably classified as containing progressive rock?

63. By November of 1978, the received wisdom of rock history would tell us that punk music had now killed progressive rock, especially in the UK. For the week of November 4th, broadly speaking, how many punk albums and how many progressive rock albums made up the Top 60 of the UK charts?

64. Which progressive rock album based its lyrics on poetry written by Nobel Prize for Literature winner Pablo Neruda?

65. At the time of writing (March 2022), which Canadian progressive rock band has had the greatest number of charting studio albums in the German album charts?

66. What do the following progressive rock albums have in common (other than being fantastic) — **Foxtrot** by *Genesis*, **Mirage** by *Camel*, **For Girls Who Grow Plump in the Night** by *Caravan*, **Backdoor Possibilities** by *Birth Control*, **Snafu** by *East of Eden*, the self-titled release from *Aardvark*, and **Script for a Jester's Tear** by *Marillion*?

67. Which progressive rock band went 50 years in between having Top 10 albums in their homeland?

68. Which progressive rock album released by a German band was a concept album based upon a poem by legendary German poet and writer Herman Hesse?

69. The British release of which album by a German progressive rock band led to a strike by the women at the record's processing plant over the cover art?

70. Which progressive rock album is a concept album depicting the events of a massacre of Native Americans which occurred in South Dakota in December 1890?

71. What band simultaneously released three different versions of the same album (that is, different versions of the songs or different tracks included on the album, not different musical formats such as CD, Vinyl, Download, etc.) when released for the first time in 2021?

72. What progressive rock band has released two albums in 2011 with an accompanying DVD "progumentary" detailing the recording of the album in question, and which two albums were they?

73. What do the albums **Present** by *Van Der Graaf Generator* (released in 2005) and the only album released by the band *Icarus* (in 1972) have in common?

74. What album released by one of the most prolific "neo-progressive rock" artists is a concept album detailing the adventures of the "Knights of the London Fog"?

75. What, seemingly coincidentally, do the self-titled albums by *Genesis* and *Dream Theater* have in common?

76. How many weeks did the self-titled debut by Canadian Prog band *Symphonic Slam* spend on the Canadian Top 100 album charts upon its release in 1976?

77. Which American progressive rock band did Peter Gabriel strongly consider using as his backup band for his 1977 debut solo album?

78. Which progressive rock band toured in support of their hit UK Top 40 album in 2017 with the first concert held in Istanbul, Turkey, and what was the name of the album in question?

79. Which flamenco progressive rock album released in 1979 managed the impressive feat of going platinum in Spain?

80. Which double-LP concept album once had a party held for it on the one-year anniversary of the lack of its release — which was attended by Spanish surrealist artist Salvador Dali?

Chapter Three — The Tracks

1. Which *King Crimson* track was originally called "Lark's Tongues in Aspic Part Five"?

2. Which 1970s star burst into tears in order to get her preferred song chosen as her first single?

3. Which famous keyboard player provided a guest appearance playing the Moog on the epic *Uriah Heep* track "July Morning"?

4. Which Kevin Ayers track features Syd Barrett on guitar in one of the earlier takes that ultimately was not used for the initial commercial release?

5. Which American television sitcom star from the 70s was the subject of the lyrics to a song about an obsessed fan, and what was the song?

6. The *Kansas* track "Journey from Mariabronn" was inspired by what novel?

7. Which is the only track by *Caravan* that features lead vocals from keyboard player David Sinclair?

8. Who is *Pallas*' song "The Ripper" about?

9. Which progressive rock track was the first to feature the prototype Moog Apollo, the first-ever polyphonic synthesizer?

10. Which song by *Muse* is about the Bilderberg Group?

11. Who was the Mike Oldfield track *Flying Start* about?

Chapter Three — The Tracks Answers? Questions!

12. What was the originally intended name for the "Karn Evil 9" suite of tracks that comprised most of *Emerson Lake & Palmer's* **Brain Salad Surgery**, before Peter Sinfield heard the music and suggested the name change?

13. Which *Renaissance* track was originally entitled "Rose of China"?

14. Which progressive rock track takes its title from an expression used on the German version of *Sesame Street*?

15. What track by *Can* managed to sell 300,000 copies when released as a single in the early 1970s?

16. *Renaissance*'s "A Trip to the Fair" was inspired by part of a date between what two individuals?

17. Although many fans have assumed that the lyrics to Pink Floyd's "Pigs (Three Different Ones)" from **Animals** take an explicit shot at American politics with the reference to the "Whitehouse" — what is the actual subject of this reference?

18. The track "Le Voleur D'Extase" by *Atoll* from their seminal **L'araignée-mal** album was brought to the band by guitarist Christian Beya, who had played this song live in a progressive rock band he was in prior to joining *Atoll*. This band, which never recorded any of their songs on vinyl, went by the old Latin name for a French city, which sounds similar to someone claiming to have ordered a certain alcoholic beverage — what was this band called?

19. Which progressive rock artist had a single in the 1980s that went to #1 on the singles chart for as many as 10 different countries?

20. "Honky Tonk Train Blues," a 1976 solo track by Keith Emerson, hit #1 in what country's singles chart on two separate occasions, for a grand total of four weeks?

21. What progressive rock track concerns a man named Mr. Glee who is imprisoned due to being fond of children?

22. *Spirit*'s guitarist Randy California guest-starred on what Peter Hammill solo album track?

23. What single was swiftly withdrawn due to concurrent terrorist activity, after having broken into the UK Top 40 singles chart?
24. What Ontario holiday is referenced in the song "Lakeside Park" by *Rush*?
25. Which progressive rock artist was the *Pink Floyd* track "Alan's Psychedelic Breakfast" reportedly referencing on **Atom Heart Mother**?
26. On which 70s progressive rock track did Phil Collins play the surdu?
27. On the track "Suicide?" which closes the album **Octoberon** by *Barclay James Harvest*, whose footsteps can be heard climbing up the stairs, simulating someone walking up to the rooftop of a building for a suicide attempt?
28. What Keith Emerson-penned track was a tribute to legendary progressive rock manager and record company owner Tony Stratton-Smith?
29. Who was the vocalist on *Pink Floyd*'s "One of These Days"?
30. "As Long as He Lies Perfectly Still" was written about which progressive rock lyricist?
31. Who was the song "Tomorrow" by *The Strawbs* (off the album **Grave New World**) written about?
32. Which progressive rock artist, who found fame in the latter half of the 1970s, played the harp on one of *Barclay James Harvest*'s albums from the early 70s?
33. In the programme guide to *Jethro Tull*'s 25th Anniversary tour, on what track do Ian Anderson and Martin Barre jokingly suggest that, if you listen hard enough, you can hear Jimmy Page waving?
34. What heavy metal band recorded a cover version of *Nektar*'s "King of Twilight"?

Chapter Three — The Tracks Answers? Questions!

35. While "Valley Girl" was Frank Zappa's only Top 40 hit in the US, in which two countries did he have a different #1 single, and what was the song in question?

36. What was the original title of "Changing States" by *Emerson, Lake & Palmer* off their 1992 album **Black Moon**?

37. From where does the name for the *King Crimson* track (and album) **Starless and Bible Black** originate?

38. Which *Jethro Tull* song managed to crack the American Top 60 and Canadian Top 85 charts in 1976?

39. What track's lyrics were only written on the morning of the song first being performed as part of a very prestigious concert which was eventually released as a live album?

40. *The Beatles*' "She Came in Through the Bathroom Window" was written about an incident at a party held at the house of which progressive rock band?

41. Which track by an American progressive rock band was originally meant to be the start of a full concept album about the Royal Canadian Mounted Police (RCMP)?

42. What was ironic about the cited reason for the *IQ* track "Wintertell" being dropped from their debut vinyl LP **Tales From the Lush Attic**?

43. For which US Top 30 hit in 1982 did Peter Hammill provide vocals?

44. What track did a member of *The Moody Blues* release with the members of *10cc* as the backing band?

45. According to one of the members of the band, how long did it take *National Health* to record the eight-second song "Phlâkatön" on their second LP, **Of Queues and Cures**?

46. Which track by a German progressive rock band managed to hit #1 on the Spanish singles chart?

47. Which track on a 1973 progressive rock concept album was about a blind barbarian princess from the north?

48. It is well known that *Pink Floyd*'s "Shine on You Crazy Diamond" was about their former bandmate Syd Barrett — what other progressive rock track released a couple of years before **Wish You Were Here**'s release was also about Syd?

49. According to Justin Hayward, which track (ironically) took *The Moody Blues* the longest time to record?

50. Which progressive rock epic track was inspired by the music written by a band member for a 1973 stage production of Shakespeare's *The Tempest*?

Chapter Three — The Tracks

Answers? Questions!

Chapter Four — The Lyrics

1. Which song includes the following lyrics: "I seem to spend my whole life shouting, perhaps I should be cool. Put on some *Caravan* and *Hatfields*, like I used to do at school," and who is the artist?

2. Which band, with a lyricist whose first language obviously isn't English, provided the following lyrics in one of their songs: "An evening of great import was very big announced"?

3. Which band released a song including the following ironic, self-referential lyrics: "They are a German band who try to play the music of *Pink Floyd*"?

4. Who sang: "Palestine's a country, or at least used to be"?

5. Who wrote the lyrics: "Ponder the mystery, the spectre of starvation and the grossness of obesity"?

6. What band came up with the following lyrics: "You've either got or you haven't got style, if you've got it, you stand out a mile. A flower's not a flower if it's wilted — a hat's not a hat 'til it's tilted"?

7. Who sang: "I'd get a size-6-rugby in my face, for not liking games that much and 'being out of place'; or get my head kicked in for liking *Yes* instead of Suzi Quatro or *The Rubettes*"?

8. Who had a double bed which was "the biggest in the city"?

9. What track includes the lyrics: "Nous Sommes du Soleil, je réveil, now I will forever rise and play!"?

Chapter Four — The Lyrics Answers? Questions!

10. Which band's only album included the lyrics: "Travelling the road of space and time, taking care not to leave any imprint behind, making sure that we cover our tracks, just a matter of fact or science fiction"?

11. Which band released a self-titled album with lyrics in their own native language which, when translated into English, are: "When you hear butterflies laugh, you know how clouds taste and lying in the moonlight you will fearlessly discover the night"?

12. What track features the lyrics: "Let us go to Church and be good-looking"?

13. What track features the lyrics: "I'm vitamin-enriched, what's more I'm absolutely wholesome. No artificial processing or anything so loathsome!"?

14. What track, from which band, contains the lyrics: "Stuff coming together, stuff that belonged; the critics said 'pretentious,' oh my god they were so wrong! (They were probably right about the rug.)"?

15. What single features the lyrics: "I found it hard to follow, my foot became confused. My facial muscles echoed the rhythms that I used"?

16. Which band had a track containing lyrics comparing their music to that of *Chicago* and the *Soft Machine*"?

17. What track features the lyrics: "You won't believe the state my engine's in, I'm leaking oil and reckon I won't make it up the hill. I should have checked my fan belt too. There's a burning smell, flippin' hell I'm pulling over to the side!"?

18. Where will one find the lyrics: "I seek forgiveness, I beg your pardons, at number 9 Mulberry Gardens"?

19. Which instrumental track from the Canterbury scene had lyrics written for it, never recorded, which exhorted the listener of the track to run around with an empty Corn Flakes box on his or her head and spit breakfast cereal all over the kitchen table?

20. What song featured the lyrics: "There's a kind of stink about blue velvet trousers. In my paisley shirt I look a jerk. And my turquoise waistcoat is quite out of sight. But oh oh my haircut looks so bad"?

21. Who charitably sang: "Oh you know that we'll be there!" and on what single?

22. Which band had a hit single by taking the words of a Kurt Vonnegut poem and setting them to music?

23. What track featured the lyrics: "Webs of concrete giving off waste dust that marks the search of an age of a thousand vast empires, sweeping away legends untold to human ears"?

24. Who sang: "He may be a Led Zeppelin, he may be all the rage, I hope Jim Page remembers when he was a younger age" and on what track?

25. What do the lyrics to "Titles" by *Barclay James Harvest*, "Happy Families" by *King Crimson*, and "Mystery Tour" by *Yes* all have in common?

26. The "lyrics" to what track by a "neo-progressive" rock band "tells the tale of unrequited herring love in East Germany in the requited time of unrequited pixies"?

27. Which band sang: "If you call this sentimental crap you'll make me mad, 'cause you know that I would not sing about some passing fad"?

28. Who said: "Is it 'numinousness,' 'numinescence,' or 'numinosity'? It's like 'luminous.' You say 'numinosity'? I do."?

29. Which track features the following vocal passage: "Adolf, we're on the air. Now, one more question: You've broken bubbles with Joseph Goebbels, you've pickled herring with Hermann Göring, you even made a mess with Rudolf Heß!"?

30. In what progressive rock track does the band singing admit that they listen with attention to *The Mothers of Invention*?

31. Which progressive rock band has a track that features the timeless, super-intellectual lyrics of: "Don't sit down on the Plexiglas toilet,

said the mama to her son. Wipe the butt clean with the paper — make it nice for everyone! But don't sit down on the Plexiglas toilet, yeah!"?

32. Which progressive rock track from the 2010s is sung from the perspective of a dead wife as her corpse is floating down the river, after having been thrown into it by her husband (causing her presumably to drown)?

33. Who said: "It's two worlds divided: rich and poor, black and white, master and servant, the living and... well... the not-quite-dead. Oh yes, that's right. The spirit world plays a large part in this story that you are about to hear."?

34. On which non-*Van Der Graf Generator* album can the following Peter Hammill lyrics be found: "Back down from the mountaintop, slack rope over Niagara Falls, hack down all the jungle that's encroaching on you"?

35. The lyrics from which progressive rock track from 1974 are all about the wizard Gandalf from J.R.R. Tolkien's *Lord of the Rings* and *The Hobbit*, without ever actually naming him?

Chapter Five — The Concerts

1. According to Steve Hackett, when Genesis played Massey Hall in Toronto in 1973, which track was greeted by a derisive heckle from an audience member who bellowed out "Sounds like fucking Beethoven!"?
2. Who played the historic Marquee Club venue on New Year's Eve, 1984?
3. Which progressive rock band played for free outside the festival fence at the famous Isle of Wight Festival, even though they weren't even on the bill?
4. Which Canadian city inspired *Roger Waters* to write *The Wall* when he spat on a fan who was climbing up onto the stage like a complete lunatic during a concert held there?
5. In what city did Genesis perform their first concert without Peter Gabriel as a member?
6. The readers of German magazine *Sounds* voted which progressive rock band as having given the best concert of 1975, finishing ahead of *Genesis, The Who, Jethro Tull,* and *Santana (*who finished in 2nd through 5th place, respectively)?
7. Which legendary progressive rock drummer, while in Toronto for a 2017 performance, was kicked off the lawn of the venue by the venue's own clueless security, being told that he had to smoke his cigarette another two feet away on the sidewalk rather than the grass?

Chapter Five — The Concerts   Answers? Questions!

8. Which eight progressive rock bands played concerts that featured in the 1977–78 season of the BBC's *Sight and Sound in Concert*?

9. Who performed a concert at the historic Maple Leaf Gardens venue in Toronto on Halloween, 1972?

10. On February 27th, 1986, *Marillion* began their first major US tour in what American city?

11. Who performed their first reunion concert at Lampeter University in Wales on May 9th, 1975?

12. Canadian progressive rock band *Saga* had a surprisingly, and atypically, poorly-attended gig in London in May 2006, with an audience of only 150 people. However, two of the audience members were members of which legendary British band?

13. Which band played their final concert as a "going concern" on October 13th, 1973 at Leicester Polytechnic University?

14. Who supported *Barclay James Harvest* on their concert tour of November and December 1972?

15. Who featured as a guest musician on *Sky*'s 1984 tour of Australia?

16. Who used to take to the stage to introduce themselves as Arnold Stirrup, the support artist for the main act playing on the night — before turning out to be a member of the main band/act?

17. Which five bands played the very first "Rock-in-Opposition" concert in March 1978, and where were they from?

18. Who opened for *Van Halen* at a concert held in Reno, Nevada in 1978?

19. For the week of December 10th, 1978, how many of the 18 concerts listed as the highest attended and highest box office receipts in the US featured progressive rock bands?

20. Who were the artists, and what albums they were they promoting, for the first two concerts Fish attended?

21. Who did his only solo performing tour supporting *PFM* in 1973?

Answers? Questions!   Chapter Five — The Concerts

22. Which German Prog band played a farewell concert on December 6th, 1989 after having played 1356 over a period of 19 years?

23. Who played his first-ever live show on Bastille Day 1979 at the Place De La Concorde in Paris?

24. Who supported *Procol Harum* on their 1968 **Shine on Brightly** tour when they played in St. Louis?

25. On August 30th, 1980, 250,000 people attended a concert held at the Reichstag at the Berlin Wall, given by which progressive rock band?

26. Which progressive rock band inadvertently caused riots on a Caribbean Island in 1981, when fans unable to get into the band's sold-out show of 10,000 violently tried to crash the venue?

27. Who made his performance debut with *Hawkwind* at the Leeds Futurama Festival on September 9th, 1979?

28. Which French progressive rock artists performed at the 1973 Reading Festival?

29. At the 1976 "Brain Festival" in Essen, Germany, which progressive rock band played as many as six encores for the audience?

30. Who performed their last concert on June 17th, 1978 at the Kohfidish Festival in Austria?

31. Which band played the first concert by a British band in the US to be broadcast live across the Atlantic, and who opened for them?

32. Which band played a concert at Ivor Wynne Stadium in Hamilton, Ontario in 1975, which was so hugely attended and caused so many problems for the locals that it caused the city council to (with rare exceptions) ban concerts being held there for the next 30 years?

33. In what country was *UK*'s **Night After Night** live album recorded?

34. Where did *Van Der Graaf Generator* play their only concert in the US during the 1970s (on the same tour where they also played five dates in Canada)?

Chapter Five — The Concerts   Answers? Questions!

35. Which two Prog bands topped the Billboard Box Office charts, as part of a triple-bill, for the week of March 19th, 1977?

36. When *Caravan* played their final gig with the Pye Hastings/Richard Coughlan/Richard Sinclair/Steve Miller line-up on July 25th, 1972, with whom did they share the bill?

37. While *Gentle Giant*'s January 1978 concert at The Golder's Green Hippodrome was recorded and broadcast live for BBC Television's *Sight and Sound in Concert*, the concert was notable for what other historical reason?

38. For the week of October 21st, 1978, which artists were responsible for five of the top six attended & revenue-generating music concerts in the US?

39. The final gig *The Soft Machine* played with Daevid Allen as a member was in San Tropez, providing the music for a play written by which famous artist?

40. Where did *Emerson, Lake & Palmer* play their first-ever concert?

46

Chapter Six — Plaudits and Pundits

1. What was the name of the idiot critic from *Melody Maker* who somehow managed to pan both **Dark Side of the Moon** and **Crime of the Century** upon their initial releases in 1973 and 1974, respectively?

2. Which rock critic was described by Professor Bill Martin in his book *Listening to the Future: The Time of Progressive Rock* with the following words: "His cynicism ran as deep as his stupidity, and it is clear that he cared no more for the working class than for anything else"?

3. Which progressive rock band won the 1989 "Fromage Award" for Worst Music video, awarded by MuchMusic (the Canadian equivalent to MTV)?

4. Which *Genesis* song won a Grammy for "Best Music Video"?

5. Which two progressive rock tracks, as of 2021, have won Grammys for "Best Rock Instrumental"?

6. Which progressive rock artist won an Oscar in 1982?

7. Which rock critic made the extremely dubious claim that "disco is a much richer musical genre than progressive rock"?

8. Which magazine dubbed *Jethro Tull*'s classic **Heavy Horses** album as "Heavy Horseshit"?

Chapter Six — Plaudits and Pundits Answers? Questions!

9. Which progressive rock band won a Juno Award (Canada's version of the Grammy's) for "Most Promising Group of the Year" (the equivalent of a "Best New Artist) award for their fourth album?

10. Proving that the critics and so-called experts who decide who wins awards often don't know jack-shit about music, the Canadian progressive rock band *Maneige*, although nominated for "Most Promising Group of the Year" in early 1976 for their work in 1975, lost the award to another band. What was the great irony about the winners of that award in March 1976?

11. Which English band was voted by the readers of *Sounds* in 1978 as "Band Most Likely to Succeed"?

12. Which member of *FM* was once nominated for the Juno Award for "Most Promising Male Vocalist," seven years and six albums into his professional career?

13. German music magazine *Musik Express* called the lyrics of what progressive rock band "twaddle"?

14. Who claimed that "If Wagner were alive today, he'd work with *King Crimson*"?

15. Which band won the 1972 "Rockortunity Knocks" competition, organized by seminal British DJ John Peel?

16. Which band won the 1975 "Brightest Hope" Award from *Melody Maker*?

17. Which band was voted the most popular American band among teenagers in the US in 1979?

18. Which album was voted "Favourite Album of the Year" for 1976 by the readers of *Melody Maker*?

19. Who did *Cashbox* rate as the 13th best vocalist of 1977, and what was the irony of this honour?

20. What album won the award for "Best Australian-Designed" Album cover for the 1975 Australian Record Awards?

21. What progressive rock album was named "Album of the Year" for 1975 by *Rolling Stone* magazine?

22. What song, on which two progressive rock lead vocalists sing, won an Ivor Novello Songwriting Award in the 1980s?

23. Which progressive rock album, which included Robert Fripp as a performer, was nominated for a Grammy Award for "Best Surround Sound Album"?

24. Which album did the German *Music Express* magazine award as the "Album of the Year" in 1970?

25. Which two progressive rock bands were recipients of the "Conamus Export Award"?

Chapter Six — Plaudits and Pundits

Chapter Seven — Progressive Rock at the Cinema

1. In the 1974 film *The Taramind Seed* (starring Omar Sharif and Julie Andrews), which famous progressive rock album can be seen behind Julie Andrews' head in several shots in a scene held at a club?

2. In the 1971 Canadian film *Face-off* (considered the Canadian equivalent of the mega-hit American film *Love Story*), starring Art Hindle & Trudy Young and a host of NHL stars from the early 70s, the two lead characters walk into a record shop in Toronto, where copies of what Canterbury Scene progressive rock album can clearly be seen for sale?

3. In which movie does Christina Ricci play a ballet dancer who dances to "Moonchild" by *King Crimson*?

4. Which 2000 film features, as part of its soundtrack, music by both *Yes* ("I've Seen All Good People" and "Roundabout") and *Jethro Tull* ("Teacher")?

5. What year is The Alan Parson Project said to have come from in the film *Austin Powers: The Spy Who Shagged Me*?

6. Who left *Tangerine Dream* shortly after the recording of the soundtrack to the 1977 William Friedkin film *Sorcerer*?

Chapter Seven — Progressive Rock at the Cinema   Answers? Questions!

7. It is well known that part of *Mike Oldfield*'s **Tubular Bells** album was used in the 1973 horror film *The Exorcist* — what sci-fi comedy film from the 1980s also featured music from this album?

8. *Rush* appear as themselves in which comedy film from the 2000s?

9. In what film does Adam Sandler claim that he caught a *Jethro Tull* reunion concert?

10. To which Elizabeth Taylor film do two members of *The Strawbs* contribute music?

11. Japanese progressive rock artist Stomu Yamashta (co-creator, with Steve Winwood and Michael Shrieve, of the supergroup *Go*) recorded music for which Robert Altman film?

12. Name the three progressive rock artists who each did one soundtrack apiece for what is loosely known as "The Three Mothers" trilogy of horror films from 1977 to 2007?

13. The 1977 disaster-suspense film *Rollercoaster* features towards the end of the film a concert performance from the band *Sparks* at an amusement park — but much earlier in the film, an amusement park patron can be seen wearing a concert t-shirt of which progressive rock band?

14. According to Michael Palin on the commentary of the DVD release, which keyboard player, who toured with and recorded on a Kevin Ayers studio album, was the inspiration for the name of a character in one of the *Monty Python* films?

15. Which two progressive rock artists wrote music for the 1985 post-apocalyptic film *She?*

16. Name the two progressive rock albums represented via their personnel in the 1963 film *The VIPs*.

17. The male dance teacher in the movie version of *Pink Floyd*'s **The Wall** is famous for playing what classic sci-fi monster?

18. What 2006 science fiction film features the music of both *Deep Purple* and *King Crimson* in its soundtrack?

19. According to Eric Idle, in addition to *Led Zeppelin,* which two progressive rock artists financed *Monty Python and the Holy Grail*?

20. Who won the (now discontinued) BAFTA Award for "Best Original Song Written for a Film," even though the song wasn't written for a film?

21. Which progressive rock artist turned down the opportunity to do the score for *2010: The Year We Make Contact* (sequel to *2001: A Space Odyssey*)?

22. Who scored the official film of the 1982 World Cup, which was won by Italy?

23. According to what prolific progressive rock artist, the art director of one of the *Star Wars* films told him that "they'd cut up the books [featuring his work] and plastered them all over the studio"?

24. Which progressive rock track opens the third *Dark Shadows* film?

25. What two progressive rock albums can be said to be represented by the personnel who made the 1981 film *The Survivor*?

26. The 2018 Steve Carell film *Beautiful Boy* features music from which 1970s American progressive rock band?

27. It is well-known that the cover art for *Emerson, Lake & Palmer's* **Brain Salad Surgery** was done by the artist, H.R. Giger, who would go on to design the xenomorph for Ridley Scott's seminal sci-fi horror film *Alien*. What other progressive rock album did Giger do the cover art for?

28. Which two progressive rock bands did Director Alejandro Jodorowsky finally line up for the soundtrack to his intended version of *Dune* (which unfortunately never made it past the pre-production stage), and which three artists had he *originally* approached?

29. Film star Dudley Moore once played piano on a track by which pre-progressive rock band?

30. Which progressive rock artist plays the synthesizer featured in the "Creature Cantina" scenes in 1977's *Star Wars*?

Chapter Seven — Progressive Rock at the Cinema

31. Film star Peter Sellers played ukulele on which track, by which progressive folk-rock band?

32. In the film *School of Rock,* which progressive rock track does Jack Black exhort one of his students to listen to as an example of how to play the keyboards?

33. Which progressive rock album cover can be seen prominently in the 1971 Dario Argento film *Four Flies on Grey Velvet?*

34. The name of *This is Spinal Tap*'s Derek Smalls was taken from the liner notes of which two progressive rock albums?

35. Speaking of *Spinal Tap,* which character from the film was played by an actual progressive rock musician?

36. Who contributed a cover version of *The Beatles* "Magical Mystery Tour" to the 1976 film *All This and World War II?*

37. Which documentary film including *King Crimson* music in its soundtrack features narration by Vincent Price?

38. Continuing with *King Crimson*'s music being used in different types of films, what 70s soft-core erotic film featured one of their tracks (without the band's knowledge or consent), and what was the track?

39. Which progressive rock keyboardist appears (uncredited) in a Jess Franco film?

40. What 80s action movie music soundtrack features keyboard work from a former member of *Greenslade,* bass playing from a then-current member of *Camel,* and percussion from a future drummer for *Jethro Tull?*

41. For which film did director Richard Donner scout locations while continuously listening to *The Alan Parson Project?*

42. Oscar and Grammy award-winning music composer Hans Zimmer performed on which album by an artist from the Canterbury Prog scene?

43. Which Canterbury-scene artist was related to Darth Vader?

44. Cinematically speaking, what do the albums **Discipline** by *King Crimson*, **The Low Spark of High-Heeled Boys** by *Traffic*, **The Yes Album** by *Yes*, and both **Apostrophe** and **Joe's Garage** by Frank Zappa have in common?

45. Which artist from a progressive rock band scored a huge international hit when his track recorded for a film in 1970 later became the theme music for a different, Best Picture Oscar-Winner?

46. Which progressive rock band's tour of California was documented and filmed by the National Film Board of Canada?

47. Which progressive rock artist recorded two songs for the 1966 Jane Fonda film *La Curée* prior to becoming famous for his rock music?

48. What two progressive rock songs have been "performed" in motion pictures over the years by comedic actor Will Ferrell?

49. Speaking of *Saturday Night Live* alumni, which two films from the 2010s starring former *SNL* cast members each feature *Argent*'s "Hold Your Head Up" as part of their movie soundtracks?

50. Which Marvel superhero actor covered half of what progressive rock classic?

Chapter Eight — Progressive Rock on Television

1. In the 1971 episode of *Doctor Who* entitled "The Mind of Evil," the Doctor's villainous arch-rival, the Master, can be seen listening to which progressive rock track?

2. What famous progressive rock album can clearly be seen on display in a scene set inside a record store in the 1978 episode of *Charlie's Angels* entitled "Angel Blues"?

3. In the 1993 series finale of the American sitcom *Cheers*, Kirstie Alley's character Rebecca Howe pretends to be both the wife of Sam (Ted Danson) and a corporate lawyer from which progressive rock-sounding law firm?

4. In the 2004 season finale of *Jonathan Creek* entitled "Gorgon's Wood," Jonathan stumbles upon a copy of which *Jethro Tull* vinyl LP, which gives him a clue to help solve a mystery?

5. *Uriah Heep*'s "Traveller in Time" is featured in an episode of which time-travelling British television show?

6. The 2021 BBC/Netflix series *The Serpent* features the use of which track by *Brainticket* as part of the incidental music?

7. After leaving *Gryphon*, recorder/crumhorn/keyboard player Richard Harvey went on to compose the theme music for the televised dramatizations of which famous detective, made and broadcast throughout the 1980s and 1990s?

Chapter Eight — Progressive Rock on Television   Answers? Questions!

8. *Steeleye Span's* lead singer Maddy Prior's father wrote episodes for which famous British science-fiction series?

9. What was the name of the fictional band said to be at the "vanguard of progressive rock" by *Jonathan Creek* in the series' episode "No Trace of Tracy"?

10. Which former *Doctor Who* script editor is thanked in the liner notes to the 1994 *Pink Floyd* album **The Division Bell**?

11. The theme tune for the 1975 *Play for Today* episode *Gangsters*, which led to a series from 1976–1978, was composed and recorded by which progressive rock band?

12. The *Emerson, Lake and Palmer* track "Tank" was featured in a deleted scene for which *Doctor Who* story?

13. Season 3 of the Christina Hendricks series *Good Girls* (NBC/Netflix 2018–2021) features in its soundtrack which track from the solo album of a member of one of the most famous progressive rock bands?

14. According to Ian Anderson, *Jethro Tull* got the inspiration for launching giant white balloons into the crowd at concerts from which classic British television series from the 1960s?

15. What was the name of the track Peter Hammill wrote in 1979 exclusively for the children's television show *Play Away*?

16. What progressive rock track was written and used for the British series *The Paper Lads*?

17. Basil Fawlty himself, John Cleese, provided the narration for the re-recording of which high-selling classic progressive rock album for its 30th anniversary in 2003?

18. The Courtroom Television Network (known as "Court TV") launched in 1991, becoming famous in 1995 for its broadcast of the O.J. Simpson Murder Trial that year. Its other most notable broadcasted civil lawsuit trial involved music — who were the plaintiffs and the defendants?

Answers? Questions!   Chapter Eight — Progressive Rock on Television

19. The German thriller television series *Das Messer* used which track from a German progressive rock band as its musical theme tune?

20. What was the favourite band of former *Doctor Who* actress Mary Tamm?

21. *Doomwatch* and *Jesus of Nazareth* star Robert Powell provided the narration to what progressive rock album from 1975?

22. Bill Oddie, one-third of television's *The Goodies*, had which track from a Canterbury Prog band inspired by, and dedicated to, him?

23. Which progressive rock band appeared on the first episode of *The David Essex Showcase* broadcast in June 1982?

24. *The New Avengers/Absolutely Fabulous* star Joanna Lumley is a distant relative of which 1970s-era progressive rock artist?

25. The 1970s science show *Don't Ask Me* featured which instrumental progressive rock track as its theme music?

26. The Steve Coogan series *Saxondale* season one, episode five, features musical extracts from which two *Jethro Tull* tracks?

27. The 12th Doctor hums the tune to which progressive rock track in the 2014 episode of *Doctor Who* entitled "The Caretaker"?

28. The *Justin Hayward* song "It Won't Be Easy" was the theme tune to which British television series?

29. Which cast member of an episode of the Canadian 1970s science-fiction series *The Starlost* worked on a *Pink Floyd* album?

30. Which progressive rock guitarist's hands feature in an episode of *Red Dwarf*?

31. Which band's performance on French television was interrupted with a news flash about the attempted assassination of Pope John Paul the II in 1981, and what track were they performing?

32. Which progressive rock singer and songwriter was so impressed with the 2007 episode of *Doctor Who* that she wrote a letter to the credited writer of the tale?

Chapter Eight — Progressive Rock on Television   Answers? Questions!

33. In 1969, *The Soft Machine* provided over an hour of music for an avant-garde multi-media show entitled *Spaced*, held at the London Roundhouse, and featuring choreographed dancing on stage by ballerinas and ex-army gymnasts. In a clip of the show, a BBC Arts television programme substituted the music of which progressive rock band to accompany the visuals?

34. *Ayreon*'s Arjen Anthony Lucassen also has a project entitled *Star One*, which is named after an episode of which British science fiction television series?

35. Which television soundtrack composer designed the appearance EMS VCS3 synthesizer, which is heard prominently on such albums as **Air Conditioning** by *Curved Air*, **Dark Side of the Moon** by *Pink Floyd*, and **Lizard** by King Crimson?

36. Music from Vangelis' album *Heaven and Hell* was used as the theme to which wildly popular science television series in 1980, still among the most widely watched PBS series in the world?

37. Which three artists appeared on the same NBC TV programme from 1970 entitled *Switched-on Symphony*?

38. Which album by *The Moody Blues* features cover art painted by an artist who painted the cover artwork for novelizations of *Doctor Who* stories?

39. In November 1995, *Jethro Tull* appeared on network television in the US on a popular talk show, wherein Ian Anderson was greatly amused that what two hosts were utterly clueless as to what a "sporran" was?

40. In a 1984 edition of the BBC series *Pop Quiz* featuring both Toyah Wilcox (and coincidentally, a question to which the answer was her future husband, Robert Fripp), which progressive rock album cover was the subject of a question given to her teammate, singer Paul Young?

Answers? Questions!   Chapter Eight — Progressive Rock on Television

41. Which 1975 progressive rock album had a novel named after it (containing one of the longest published sentences in English literature at 13,955 words in length), which was turned into both a radio play and a television adaptation for the BBC?

42. What progressive rock track did the German TV channel ZDF use as the theme music for their popular current affairs programme *Aspekte*?

43. The theme tune to the BBC2 programme *Out of Court* (which investigated the British courts, lawyers, and the law) was composed by a former member of what 70s British progressive rock band?

44. Which progressive rock band faced an outcry for their appearance on *The Old Grey Whistle Test* from claims that "Whispering" Bob Harris (the show's host) had used his influence to get a band a slot on the programme?

45. Who cited *Monty Python's Flying Circus* as an example of "prog humour"?

46. *Audience*'s "I Had a Dream" and *Barclay James Harvest*'s "When the City Sleeps" were both featured in the soundtrack to the second season of which British television series?

47. What do the Frank Zappa tracks "I'm the Slime," "Dancin' Fool," "Rollo," "Peaches En Regalia," and "The Meek Shall Inherit Nothing" have in common?

48. "Carry On Wayward Son" by *Kansas* was used as the opening music for the season finale of each season (except for its first) of which American television drama?

49. Which progressive rock band performed the soundtrack to the Japanese show *Cromartie High School*?

50. The original drummer for which German progressive rock band left before recording their first album but rose to modest fame over 15 years later as the host of a striptease show on German television?

Chapter Nine — Prog Rock Quotes

Who said:

1. "Sorry *Radiohead*, but you're as prog as they come."

2. "This isn't *Jethro Tull*, it's shit!"

3. "I think punk was a youth culture that wasn't particularly anything to do with music. It was an excuse for badly performed and executed hard rock."

4. "Champagne is my shampoo."

5. "From 1975, we were considered Germany's answer to *Genesis* and *King Crimson*."

6. "I've played some shit venues in my time, including the Zoom Club in Frankfurt where there are no doors on the toilets to discourage heroin users from shooting up, the Mobileritz in Antwerp, frequented mainly by transvestites who ignore the band but cheer the blue slideshow on afterwards."

7. "He was Darth Vader, I was Obi-Wan Kenobi!"

8. "I've always thought of *FM* as Canada's quintessential Prog band."

9. "He thought we were a bunch of little white shits playing this unfunky, cerebral caterwauling."

10. "If this band makes it, I'll have to commit suicide."

11. "In those days in our live show, we usually alienated 50 percent of the audience to the extent that they would walk out."

12. "If you're not a pop star, you're still the asshole."

13. "Seeing Keith Emerson in *ELP* destroying a keyboard with knives was infinitely cooler than going to see *The Eagles*."

14. "1975 was a difficult year to be a thinking rock musician. The halcyon days of progressive rock, when musicians were actually encouraged to be creative and original, were over, and the music industry had gone into a horrid kind of two-year gestation period which was to end with the birth of punk. In other words, at the exact point when the British rock business and media were beginning to turn their backs on decent music and gearing themselves up to promote instead some of the most crass, simplistic, brutal, ugly music imaginable, in an atmosphere where an admitted inability to play one's own instrument was hailed as a sign of genius..."

15. "I was just about to hit the road for India when I joined, I've got practically no musical knowledge."

16. "Deaf Idiot Journalist Starts Beatle Rumour."

17. "**Atom Heart Mother** is a good case, I think, for being thrown into the dustbin and never listened to by anyone ever again!"

18. "It's bloody *Curved Air*!"

19. "The American Press invented this hype, and when they found out this hype was full of baloney, they blamed us."

20. "There is information I need to impart to you. You can get it in one of two ways. One takes a minute or so, the other takes several years. Which do you prefer?"

21. "I don't like hippies, and I'm usually rather put off by naked ladies unless the time is right. Well, indeed, unless the money's right."

22. "When I came back... they were already living in a commune. Two weeks later I moved in. They had already started to make music,

but it was only a thing for men. Women weren't allowed to make music."

23. "To write a Prog album, you've got to sit in traffic jams and go through a lot of shit before you get to the studio, and then you come up with the goods."

24. "Jimmy Page used to show us Polaroids involving close-up blurred parts of young ladies' anatomy, often featuring soft fruit — that seemed to be in quite a lot of these photographs."

25. "The festival in Holland was the biggest gig we did at that time. We played to an audience of about 250,000 people. Although, only 10,000 of whom were awake."

26. "You need another fucking Aqualung!"

27. "It was an extremely dull grammar school and I can't remember a single stimulating thing about Canterbury."

28. "We had nothing to do with those things. The other bands were devoted to the god of money, but we were alone, isolated, even badly seen by many and we saw all the others very badly. We thought they were scoundrels who had allowed themselves to be put in their underwear by power."

29. "There would have been no point in us droning on like *The Moody Blues*."

30. "I want people around me who are creative, lively, interested and interesting. Dave is none of those things."

31. "People were lying on the floor, dazed. It was all too much for some people — fragile young minds, made even more fragile by drug taking and this music."

32. "Music will never be the same as it was back then. The seventies was the last era when the musicians were ahead of the technology."

33. "It was absolutely fucking frightening, satanic... designed to shock."

34. "The bastions at the NME at least thought they had killed it. Then we broke out and it was like 'Hey, we thought you bastards were dead.'"

35. "The first cassette I received from Arista went out the limo window after about fifteen minutes. The next one went out the hotel window."

36. "*Spandau Ballet, Visage, Ultravox...* there's some good music going down. The thing I really like is that the bands concerned are being highly creative. They're applying feel to technology with synthesis and it all sounds really positive, really progressive."

37. "I don't think *Focus* are Prog rock, but lots of others do."

38. "*Pink Floyd* were our rivals, and when 'Arnold Layne' came out, I thought 'Fuck, that's so good.'"

39. "We were very competitive. We were always be looking at up and coming bands like *Yes* and wanting to do better."

40. "This is where *Pink Floyd* have scored. They can re-form whenever they like — with or without the full complement of players. You either like those slow, ponderous, introverted atmospheric songs, or you don't."

41. "If I had known then that he would end up writing for *Bucks Fizz*, I would have hit him."

42. "None. The thought is quite hideous. I don't even think a one-off would work. The idea of having to re-learn my parts is daunting, but I suppose, perfectly possible. What would be the point though? It's over."

43. "Yes, I heard it recently. Hilarious. They play all the heavy bits and none of the tricky stuff!"

44. "Other bands with one drummer are ten times better than you with two drummers!"

45. "There's something really inventive about the Sylvester McCoy and Colin Baker-era shows that the new series, which has a much

bigger budget, really lacks. When I was growing up in El Paso, it was *Doctor Who* on PBS that kept me sane."

46. "If you take a mistake as a mistake, you don't get very far with improvisation. If you take a mistake as music as well, you get your ideas from the mistakes."

47. "I've worked with Rick a few times. His arrangements are beautiful. Prog has an energy about it that attracts your eye and ear."

48. "Although the vocals are very nice, they completely ruin the song, because there is too much happening — a complete battle between the vocals and the music all the way through."

49. "He really immersed himself in the story and spent weeks rewriting the narration. At first I was unsure because there were lots of 'fucks' in there but it was so cool."

50. "I'm a fan and his playing on the track is what we heard in our minds' eye imagination. He blew me away. He literally blew me away."

51. "They were very weird compared to everyone else and well into avant-garde jazz... it sounded like utter gibberish to me — when I first heard it, I thought 'What the fuck is that?'"

52. "In the old days, I wrote a lot of nice lyrics about little flowers and forests, but in the meantime I have become older and seen what has become of music. There really are some stupid people out there trying to tell the world how much fun it is to be in the navy."

53. "He opened me up, made me more courageous. Suddenly it wasn't all drum magazines, but using the instrument to put your own character across."

54. "It is clear that he is by far the best product of, the most exotic and the great genius of the Canterbury musicians. I would say for sure he's head and shoulders above everybody."

55. "I think someone ought to tell you you're really a hopeless musician. But would you like to write some lyrics?"

Chapter Nine — Prog Rock Quotes Answers? Questions!

56. "Guitarist/writer seeks receptive musicians determined to strive beyond existing stagnant music forms."

57. "You can take your fucking record and shove it up your ass!" *[to Steve Howe]*

58. "It was always cool. It was just never hip." *[in response to being asked whether Prog rock was ever cool]*

59. "The British Press definitely wanted the death of Prog, I think, because they were uncomfortable with dealing with musicians who were more intelligent than they were."

60. "It's amazing how many people think they can write! It's amazing how evil music is when put in the wrong hands!"

61. "At last, the new collection of songs you have not really been waiting for." *[in an album's liner notes]*

62. When asked in a TV interview why *Gong* was leaving their hippy commune located in a house in the midst of a "magical forest" 150km south of Paris to go live in England, what was Daevid Allen's response?

Chapter Ten — Miscellaneous

1. For what year did the members of *Metallica* thank *Jethro Tull* for not releasing an album?

2. While Phil Collins plays drums on the *Band Aid* November 1984 charity single "Do They Know It's Christmas," which two progressive rock legends appeared on the charity single by *Who Cares* that was released just a few months later in March 1985?

3. In the 1950s, Daevid Allen (later of *Gong*) performed at the same theatre in Australia, around the same time, as which famous television talk show host?

4. Which famous progressive rock frontman told DJ Joey Vendetta in 1994 that his fondest memory of playing in Toronto over the years was the city's population of black squirrels?

5. Which former Prog band keyboard player, after leaving the band, played on each of *The Bee Gees* tracks on the **Saturday Night Fever** album?

6. Sci-fi book cover artist Chris Achilleos designed the costume worn by which star for a 1980 music video?

7. Who allegedly (and metaphorically) "shit his pants" after seeing how incredible a guitarist Allan Holdsworth was when performing for *U.K.* in the US in 1978?

8. Which progressive rock artist from the 1970s would later play a significant role in *Bon Jovi* making it big?

9. 1977 is generally considered by rock historians and critics to be the year that punk exploded and came to mainstream success, allegedly "killing" progressive rock that same year. How true this is, based on historical facts and information, is of some debate, especially outside the UK. The RPM Weekly album charts for Canada for the week of May 28th, 1977 (well after many seminal punk albums had been released already by the likes of *The Clash, The Damned,* and *The Jam*) list as many as eight bands that could reasonably be considered progressive rock bands in the Top 50 (*Supertramp* at #4 with **Even in the Quietest Moments**; *ELO* at #8 with **New World Record**; *Jethro Tull* at #9 with **Songs From the Wood**; *Emerson, Lake & Palmer* at #26 with **Works Volume 1**; *Kansas* at #30 with **Leftoverture**; *Manfred Mann's Earth Band* at #32 with **The Roaring Silence**; *Genesis* at #38 with **Wind and Wuthering**; and *Klaatu* at #43 with **3:47 E.S.T.**). How many punk bands featured in the Top 50 that week?

10. *King Crimson, ELP,* and *PFM* lyricist Peter Sinfield wrote what song which became a #1 hit in eight different countries?

11. Which progressive rock artist has spent much of his life living in a windmill in France?

12. Which progressive rock artist appeared in *Playboy* in May 1983?

13. Which Italian progressive rock artist met the woman he would go on to marry as she was working as a waitress in Italy, after having her money stolen from her shortly after arriving in that country?

14. Which progressive rock artist wrote the lyrics to *Nena*'s 1983 smash pop hit "99 Luftballoons"

15. English Snooker star Steve Davis was such a huge fan of what progressive band that he helped to fund their tour of the UK in 1988?

16. Which band turned down the suggestion from one of its members to do a concept album based upon *The Little Prince*?

17. Reginald Dwight took his much more famous first name from which member of a progressive rock band?

18. Although *Klaatu* were accused of being *The Beatles* recording under a pseudonym, which British progressive rock artists once deliberately recorded under the name *The Moles* as part of a marketing plan to make people think they were *The Beatles*?

19. What band had a tour funded by the Communist Party of a certain country, which was met in response by the Fascist Party of the same country stealing the band's van and all of their gear during the tour?

20. Which band, during their 1974 US tour, noticed a young teenage Michael Jackson sitting in the front row of the audience?

21. When promoting his 1992 solo album **Amused to Death**, Roger Waters suggested on radio that with *Phantom of the Opera*, Andrew Lloyd Webber had ripped off which *Pink Floyd* track, which he claimed he had written 15 years earlier?

22. What was the reason that *King Crimson* divided up their lengthier tracks on their first album into parts?

23. Who sued *Jethro Tull* in 1971 for "inappropriate copyright infringement"?

24. What Frank Zappa alumni performed on "We Are the World" by *USA For Africa*?

25. Who once claimed on television that *Hawkwind* should have written (presumably the music for) *Star Wars*?

26. Which famous 1980s pop singer auditioned unsuccessfully for *Manfred Mann Chapter Three*, the successor band to *Manfred Mann* and the precursor to *Manfred Mann's Earth Band*?

27. In London in 2007, Swedish Prog band *The Flower* Kings, upon returning to that evening's scheduled venue (following an Asian dinner after their late soundcheck), encountered which legendary progressive rock artist in the midst of acquiring tickets for their show that evening?

28. Band-personnel wise, what do *Renaissance, Gong, Yes*, and the *Soft Machine* have in common?

Chapter Ten — Miscellaneous　　　　　　　　　　　　Answers? Questions!

29. What band's debut album, when played on the radio in Cleveland, caused the radio station in question to be inundated with callers asking when the new *Led Zeppelin* album (that they assumed they had just heard a track from) was going to be released?

30. According to *Magma*'s original bassist Laurent Thibault, the band's destiny to play only the music of the "Magma Orchestra" going forward was set when an enthusiastic American jumped onto a table at an early gig at a club and proclaimed that *Magma* was "the greatest band in the world." Given that *Magma* are a French band who sing in an invented language of Kobian, what language were these words apparently shouted in, according to Thibault?

31. In what city in continental Europe will you find "Frank Zappa Street"?

32. Which legendary producer of a plethora of classic progressive rock albums from the 1970s later became *Monty Python*'s financial manager?

33. Believe it or not, the first live concert ever attended by pop singer Rick Astley (of "Never Going to Give You Up" fame) was of which progressive rock band, which apparently "blew his mind"?

34. According to Ian Anderson, which *Jethro Tull* song was used by American forces to help flush out Panamanian dictator Manuel Noriega from his hiding spot, when they played rock music at him at an extremely high volume?

35. Which star of *Ghostbusters* went to grade school with a progressive rock bassist?

SIDE TWO:
Questions?
Answers!

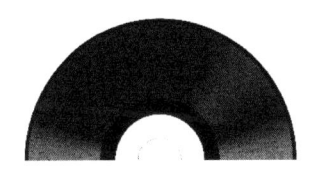

Chapter Eleven — The Artists

Part A — British Progressive Rock

1. Keith Emerson.
2. *Fuzzy Duck*.
3. *Jethro Tull*. Tull were in between guitarists in late 1968 when they were invited to be included in *The Rolling Stones* **Rock and Roll Circus** concert video (recorded on a circus stage). It was meant to be aired on the BBC, but the *Stones* didn't release it until 1996.
4. *The Strawbs*.
5. Phil Collins.
6. *King Crimson*.
7. *King Crimson*.
8. David Gilmour of *Pink Floyd*.
9. Keith Emerson, then of *The Nice*. The *Emerson, Lake and Palmer* album **Live at the Royal Albert Hall** was released in 1993 from concerts held there as part of the band's 1992–1993 World Tour, by which point either everything had been forgiven or forgotten, or maybe the venue didn't realize who Keith Emerson was.
10. *Druid*.
11. David Jackson of *Van Der Graaf Generator*.

Chapter Eleven — The Artists   Questions? Answers!

12. *Genesis.* Peter Gabriel heard the interview and mentioned this to the other members of the band, which gave them all a shot of confidence.
13. Real Estate Agent.
14. *Supertramp.*
15. Mel Collins, of *King Crimson* and *Camel* fame.
16. *Supertramp*'s John Anthony Helliwell.
17. 14.
18. *King Crimson.*
19. Clergyman. *Fruupp* would record one more album, *Modern Masquerades*, after Houston's departure.
20. Vangelis. The *Aprhrodite's Child* keyboardist had auditioned to join *Yes* at Jon Anderson's suggestion, but he ultimately declined due to problems obtaining a work Visa and a reluctance to travel for the purposes of touring. Jon and Vangelis would of course work together as *Jon and Vangelis* (go figure!) in the early 1980s, with Anderson also making an appearance on Vangelis' 1975 album **Heaven and Hell**.
21. Robert Fripp of *King Crimson.*
22. Robert Fripp of *King Crimson.* The track in question was "The Devil's Triangle" off **In the Wake of Poseidon.**
23. Robert Calvert of *Hawkwind.*
24. Producer Tony Clarke. It was hoped that the press wouldn't notice that he wasn't actually Mike Pinder, or that there were only four members of the band present for their comeback launch party.
25. David Bowie.
26. *The Enid.* The track in question was a 19-minute version of "Fand." The band had effectively disbanded in 1980 when their record company had gone bankrupt, but the response to the track

from the British public was so overwhelmingly positive that it led to the band reforming and releasing new albums starting in 1983.

27. *Renaissance.* The guitarist in question was Michael Dunford and the poet (or "poetess" as she is sometimes referred to in the literature) was Betty Thatcher (no relation to Margaret, as far as we know).

28. Ex *Yes* and (Led) *Zeppelin.* Only four demos were written and recorded and have, at the time of writing, not been commercially released.

29. Peter Sinfield of *King Crimson* (who would also work with *Emerson, Lake & Palmer* and *Premiata Forneria Marconi*).

30. John Lodge of *The Moody Blues.* And no, I don't understand what he's talking about either.

31. *Curved Air.* Of the original members of the band, only lead singer Sonja Kristina had not been in *Sisyphus.*

32. Van Driver, somewhat ironically given the name of the band he was in. We are of course referring to David Jackson the saxophone player, not David Jackson the actor who was playing Gan on *Blake's Seven* at this time.

33. Gryphon.

34. *Hawkwind.* The charges concerned unpaid taxes.

35. Jethro Tull.

36. *Ramases,* who released two albums in the 1970s, including the 1971 release **Space Hymns** which all four of Godley, Creme, Stewart, and Gouldman played on.

37. *Ramases* — he adopted his name after claiming to have been visited by the spirit of the Egyptian Pharaoh Ramesses while driving his car in Sheffield (which is just the sort of place that the spirits of Egyptian Pharaohs are known to be hanging around). Ramases began dressing and behaving in an eccentric manner, wearing silk robes, and shaving his head, in the style of the Yul Brynner from *The Ten Commandments.*

38. *Gentle Giant.* Under his real name, Reginald Dwight, Elton had played on a tour with the members of *Gentle Giant* in their previous band, *Simon Dupree and the Big Sound*. John had wanted to join *Gentle Giant,* but the band members specifically didn't want any sort of commercial sound for their band.
39. Annie Haslam of *Renaissance.*
40. *Camel* for the album **Mirage**. The FM Action chart was designed to track albums that had the most radio airplay on the US's "progressive" stations (which did not necessarily mean progressive rock stations). That particular week, **Red** by *King Crimson* was #6, **There's the Rub** by *Wishbone Ash* was #7, **Pinafore Days** by *Stackridge* was tied for 10th, **Spyglass Quest** by *Greenslade* was tied for #14 and **Red Queen to Gryphon Three** by *Gryphon* was tied for #19th spot.

Part B — The Canterbury Scene

41. Steve Hillage, Clive Brooks, Mont Campbell and Dave Stewart, who recorded an album under the moniker *Arzachel*. The quartet had started out as *Uriel* before Brooks, Campbell and Stewart would go on to call themselves *Egg*.
42. Didier Malherbe.
43. **Sweet Deceiver** by Kevin Ayers.
44. Daevid Allen, who was a member of the band before being barred from re-entering the UK by immigration authorities, forcing him to stay in France where he would form *Gong*.
45. *Lindisfarne, Status Quo,* and *Slade!*
46. Richard Sinclair (who had been a member of *Caravan, Hatfield and the North* and *Camel* during the decade).
47. *Soft Machine.*
48. Gilli Smyth of *Gong* (as well as the poet known as Lady June).
49. Pye Hastings of *Caravan.*

50. Mont Campbell of *Egg* and *National Health*.
51. Mike Howlett, bass player for *Gong*.
52. Kevin Ayers with **The Confessions of Dr. Dream and Other Stories**. If that wasn't impressive enough, the **June 1, 1974** live album that he contributed several songs to (and was credited as a joint artist on, along with John Cale, Nico, and Eno) was #3 in Belgium that week.
53. Diester Gewissler. He performed live with the band including playing on their performance of "Dreaming It" (a track which was never studio-recorded for an album) for French television for the programme *Jazz Land* broadcast May 8th, 1971.

Part C — Italian Progressive Rock

54. *Maxophone*. The B-side to their 1977 single was entitled "Cono Di Gelato" and for decades was their final recorded work.
55. Peter Hammill.
56. *PFM* (as *Premiata Forneria Marconi* had then become known as internationally).
57. *Delirium*. Their track "Jesahel" was #1 for the weeks of March 18th through to the week of April 22nd.
58. I Dreamed of Electric Sheep released by *PFM* in 2021.
59. *Sensations Fix*.
60. "Profondo Rosso," in November and December 1975.
61. A. *Banco Del Mutuo Soccorso* — the album being their self-titled debut which includes "Il giardino del mago" as the lengthiest (18 minutes and 36 seconds long) and "Passagio," the shortest at one minute and 19 seconds). The claim is made in the liner notes to their 2019 album **Transiberiana** album. There are some tracks by *Goblin* (notably the concluding track on the **Zombi** album — also known as the **Dawn of the Dead** soundtrack) which are shorter than Passagio so, without getting into the debate of what

counts as "Prog," perhaps "excluding soundtracks" should be added as a qualifier?

62. **Palepoli** by *Osanna*.

63. *I Giganti* with the 1971 album **Terra in Boca**.

64. *La Maschera Di Sera*, who released the album *Le Porte Del Domani* in 2013 (while also simultaneously releasing an English-language version, **The Gates of Tomorrow**).

Part D — German Progressive Rock

65. Helmut Köllen, former Bass player for *Triumvirat*, who accidentally killed himself from Carbon Monoxide poisoning in May 1977 when listening to tapes of his forthcoming solo album in his car.

66. *Grobschnitt*.

67. *Triumvirat*. The CD release for **Illusions on a Double Dimple** claims that it reached the Top 40, but there are a couple of caveats to this. *Nektar* had previously made the US Top 40 in 1973 with **Remember the Future** but some may not count them as German as they were a British band based in Germany. Note as well that according to other sources (including Wikipedia), **Illusions on a Double Dimple** only made it to #55, although the follow-up, 1975's **Spartacus** by all accounts hit #27, so *Triumvirat* likely still hold the record absent any German rock bands and by counting *Nektar* as British. Incidentally, *Triumvirat's* **Old Loves Die Hard** made #30 in Canada when released in 1976.

68. *Eloy*. The band's farewell was short-lived as they would be back with another album by 1988.

69. *Novalis*. The album in question was 1985's **Nach uns die Flut**, released at a time when the German music press were pressing (pun intended) the band to become more commercial and modern-sounding rather than staying true to themselves. The band chose to call it quits rather than compromise or change their musical sound.

70. *Jane* — the live album **Live At Home** was a double-LP released in 1977 and broadcast on national German radio in January of that year.

71. *Anyone's Daughter*, taken from the song of the same name from the album **Fireball**.

72. *Tangerine Dream* with **Rubycon**.

73. *Amon Duul II*, specifically for their 1975 double-album **Made In Germany**, a concept album about German history of the 19th and 20th centuries.

74. *Agitation Free.*

Part E — North American Progressive Rock

75. Buttonville (part of the Town of Markham).

76. *Crack the Sky.*

77. Geddy Lee.

78. Jon Anderson of *Yes.*

79. *Styx.*

80. *Kansas* (Don Kirshner signed Kansas to his own new label in 1974 after having created *The Monkees* for television in 1966).

81. Nash the Slash. The original member of the Canadian Prog band *FM* also had a substantial solo career.

82. They first had a smash hit single in Puerto Rico with their song "Humble Stance," while, at the time of writing, each of the band's last 14 studio albums charted in Germany (with each of the last three — **20/20, Sagacity** and **Symmetry** reaching the Top 20 there).

83. Nash the Slash, who never allowed any guitars on his solo work. Gilmour had offered to play guitar on Nash's album **Children of the Night** which was produced by none other than Steve Hillage.

84. Kerry Livgren of *Kansas*.

85. *Hush*.

86. "Don't Pay the Ferryman" by Chris De Burgh.

Part F — Progressive Rock From the Rest of Europe

87. *IQ*. In the liner notes to the CD, they also indicate that the track was inspired by *IQ*.

88. *Tai Phong*, which included Jean-Jacques Goldman on guitar and vocals. Goldman was the predominant songwriter and co-producer of French-Canadian singer Celine Dion's **D'eux** album in 1995.

89. *Magma*. The drummer in question being Christian Vander.

90. "Tramdriver," released as a single in November 1975.

91. *SBB* from Poland. At the time they were known as *Niemen* as they performed with legendary Polish musician Czesław Niemen at the time.

92. *Atoll*.

93. Bo Hansson, who scored a major hit worldwide with his album **Music Inspired By Lord of the Rings**, which made the Top 40 in the UK and went Gold both there and in Australia, and whose song "Tax Free" was recorded by Hendrix.

94. Forever Blowing Bubbles by *Clearlight*.

95. **Earth and Fire**. The Dutch band eventually morphed into a pop band by the end of that decade, but most of their Top 10 hit singles came when they were an out-and-out progressive rock band.

96. *Igra Staklenih Perli* which is Serbian for The Glass Bead Game.

97. *Pulsar*. Their second album, **The Strands of the Future**, had sold 40,000 copies within six months of its release in 1976.

98. *Popol Ace*, who were originally called *Popol Vuh*. The more famous German band by that name had been releasing albums since 1970, a couple of years before the Norwegian band had formed, so they did the honourable thing and changed their name to avoid confusion in the marketplace once they became aware of their German namesakes.
99. *Atoll*'s lead singer, Andre Balzer.
100. *Opeth*, whose 2016 album **Sorceress** rode to the top of the album charts in Germany that year. The band previously had two albums hit number one in a Scandinavian country — not their homeland, but in their neighbouring country of Finland.
101. Christian Decamps of *Ange*.
102. *Focus*. The two singles in question were "Sylvia" and a faster-paced version of "Hocus Pocus" (called "Hocus Pocus 2" by some).
103. *Magma*'s drummer and bandleader, Christian Vander.
104. *Korni Grupa*, with the track "Generacija '42," which was the entry for the former Yugoslavia in the 1974 contest. The track lost out to ABBA who won for "Waterloo." The band would subsequently release an English-language version of the track, entitled "Generation 42" on their next album **Not An Ordinary Life**, which featured English vocals throughout the album.

Part G — Prog From the Rest of the World

105. *Far East Family Band* (which featured future New Age artist Kitaro in its ranks).
106. *Témpano*, Venezuela's best-known progressive rock band which formed in the late 70s and released six albums in the 1980s before they reformed in 1999 for *El Fin De La Infancia* (which translates to "Childhood's End"), on which Pejtsik played cello.
107. *Sebastian Hardie*.

108. Julian Jay Savarin, who was born in Dominica. The first album, **A Time Before This** was released under the name *Julian's Treatment* while the second album, **Waiters of the Dance** (which is also the name of the first book in the *Lemmus: A Time Odyssey* sci-fi trilogy) was released under Savarin's own name.

109. *Sui Generis* from Argentina, with the influential album **Pequeñas anécdotas sobre las instituciones** (translated as "Little Anecdotes About the Institutions") — primarily a progressive folk rock album, it is one of the earliest examples of a progressive rock style seen in a major South American rock band.

110. Alemendra.

Chapter Twelve — The Albums

1. Tony Banks. The first Steven Hackett solo album featured Phil Collins on drums and Mike Rutherford on bass (the latter also having co-written with Hackett the closing track "Shadow of the Hierophant").
2. Robert Fripp.
3. **Tubular Bells** by *Mike Oldfield*.
4. **Let it Be** by *The Beatles*, **Bridge Over Troubled Water** by *Simon and Garfunkel* and **McCartney** by *Paul McCartney*.
5. Nick Mason (who co-produced **Green**).
6. 279.
7. **Phantasmagoria** by *Curved Air*.
8. **Ashes are Burning** by *Renaissance*, which is referenced in the lyrics to "Lords of the Backstage" off the #1 charting album **Misplaced Childhood** by neo-prog band *Marillion*.
9. **Free Hand**, which reached #48 in 1975. In Canada, the album managed to reach #41.
10. 1981. An album going Silver in the UK means it has achieved 60,000 sales.
11. "Toys in the Attic." *Aerosmith* released an album with the same name after *Caravan* had recorded, but not released, the tracks that would comprise the **Cunning Stunts** album.

12. **Living in the Past** by *Jethro Tull* (which itself had spent two weeks at #1 on the Canadian charts in late 1972).

13. The US and Canada. The Canada performance occurred first, on August 22nd, 1974 in Toronto, but the country was seemingly deemed unworthy by the record company of being of interest to the people of Italy.

14. **Pawn Hearts** by *Van Der Graaf Generator*

15. **Ocean** by *Eloy*, released in December 1977. The band's follow up, **Silent Cries and Mighty Echoes**, released in 1979, sold even more copies (and presumably outsold any new *Genesis* and *Queen* albums that year in Germany again, since those two bands didn't release a new album in 1979).

16. **In the Court of the Crimson King** by *King Crimson*.

17. #114.

18. Atlanto.

19. **Mechanical Moonbeams**, released in 1978, which initially went Gold and then went Platinum.

20. *Genesis*. Their album in the charts that week was not **The Lamb Lies Down on Broadway**, as one might have expected, but their debut 1969 album **From Genesis to Revelation** which that week had reached #170 in its third week in the charts in a row. The other Prog albums in the charts that week were **Welcome Back My Friends to the Show That Never Ends** (at #4) and **Brain Salad Surgery** (enjoying its 46th week on the charts at #163) by *ELP*, **When the Eagle Flies** by *Traffic* at #17, **Remember the Future** by *Nektar* at #40, **Apostrophe** by Frank Zappa at #48 with another Zappa album, **Roxy & Elsewhere** at #57, **Illusions on a Double Dimple** by *Triumvirat* at #58, **Eldorado** by *ELO* at #59, **Journey to the Centre of the Earth** by Rick Wakeman at #61 (we can blame someone named Phoebe Snow who charted at #60 for breaking up what would have been four in a row for Prog rock albums), **Hamburger Concerto** by *Focus* at #66, **Hergest Ridge** by Mike Oldfield at #87, **War**

Child by *Jethro Tull* at #96 (its first week on the charts — it would eventually hit #2), **Turn of the Cards** by *Renaissance* at #102, **The Power and the Glory** by *Gentle Giant* at #112, **Hall of the Mountain Grill** by *Hawkwind* at #119 and the debut album by *Rush* at #134.

21. **Flags**, the 1985 album released by Patrick Moraz and Bill Bruford, the cover art for which features the two men performing judo.

22. Canada, where it hit #10 on the charts the week of June 5th, 1982.

23. Rick Wakeman, because every time he listens to the album, it brings tears to his eyes.

24. **Live at Carnegie Hall** which hit #44 in the summer of 1976. In terms of studio albums, it would be *A Song for All Seasons* which got to #45 in 1978.

25. **Wish You Were Here** by *Pink Floyd* and **Gone to Earth** by *Barclay James Harvest*.

26. **Living in the Past** by *Jethro Tull* (#1), **Seventh Sojourn** by *The Moody Blues* (#4), **Close to the Edge** by *Yes* (#8), **Days of Future Passed** by *The Moody Blues* (#10). For the record, **Trilogy** by *Emerson, Lake & Palmer* was at #18 that week. Other Prog albums in the Top 100 that week included **Demons and Wizards** by *Uriah Heep* at #48, **Purple Passages** by *Deep Purple* at #52, **Thick as a Brick** by *Jethro Tull* at #57, and **The Magician's Birthday** by *Uriah Heep* entering the Top 100 chart that week at #97.

27. **Sommerabend**.

28. *Family* with their 1968 debut album **Music in a Doll's House**, which was released a couple of months before *The White Album* and was successful enough (cracking the UK Top 40) to persuade *The Beatles* to change their naming plans.

29. Mike Oldfield's **Tubular Bells**.

30. **Merry-Go-Round** by *Grobschnitt*. The cover art to the 1979 album depicted the contents of every song on the LP, including *The Village People* who *Grobschnitt* satirize in their track "A.C.Y.M."

31. *Focus*, with **Moving Waves** at #36, **Focus 3** at #67, and **In and Out of Focus** at #71. Other Prog albums in the charts that week include **Made in Japan** by *Deep Purple* at #6, **Six Wives of Henry VIII** by Rick Wakeman at #29, **Yessongs** by *Yes* at #31, **ELO II** by *The Electric Light Orchestra* at #38, **Live** by *Uriah Heep* at #57, **The Yes Album** by *Yes* (re-entering the charts #75, interestingly for an album released in 1971), and **Who Do We Think We Are** by *Deep Purple* at #80.

32. **L,** which managed to hit the Top 10 in 1976.

33. **Stationary Traveller** by *Camel*. Technically speaking the term used is "Nosh," which is British slang for food.

34. **Phantom of the Night** by *Kayak*. The album hit the top of the charts in Holland that year.

35. **Ege Bamyashi** by *Can*. The chess sessions were played between Damo Suzuki and Irmin Schmidt.

36. Derek Shulman, lead vocalist for *Gentle Giant*.

37. **Twelfth Night**, with their live album **Live and Let Live** (as opposed to *Live and Let Die*).

38. The artwork for both albums were done by the lead vocalist of their respective bands. This doesn't technically apply for the first release of **Üdü Wüdü** as the cover art being painted by vocalist Klaus Blasquiz was not ready in time, but it has been used for every subsequent release on vinyl and CD.

39. **Contamination** by *RDM*.

40. *Atoll* for their 1975 album **L'araignée-mal**.

41. *The Alan Parsons Project* with **Eye in the Sky** and *Barclay James Harvest* with **Berlin — A Concert for the People**.

42. **Air Conditioning** by *Curved Air*.

43. **Uomo Di Pezza** by *Le Orme*.
44. **Live at Home** by *Jane*.
45. **Hall of the Mountain Grill** by *Hawkwind*.
46. **Tilt** by *Arti E Mestieri*.
47. *Manfred Mann's Earth Band* with their 1973 album **The Good Earth**.
48. **Three Friends** by *Gentle Giant*.
49. **The Power and the Passion** by *Eloy*.
50. *Pink Floyd*.
51. **Beginnings** by Steve Howe. Graeme Taylor and David Oberle played on "The Nature of the Sea." *Gryphon* had previously toured with *Yes* which no doubt fostered the connection between its two members and Howe.
52. **Cunning Stunts** (in 1975) and **Blind Dog at St. Dunstan's** (in 1976).
53. 60%. Four songs out of ten were co-written with then-current Tull member Peter-John Vettese.
54. **And Then There Were Three** by *Genesis* (appropriately enough at #3), **The Kick Inside** by Kate Bush, and **Zappa in New York** by Frank Zappa at #6.
55. They are both literally/truly solo albums by their respective artists, as Anderson and Winwood play all the instruments for each of their respective albums and perform the vocals.
56. The "Best of" collection **Strictly Commercial**, which was released in 1995 two years after his death, and which was subject to a lawsuit from Frank's wife Gail Zappa against Rykodisc for allegedly having released versions of some of the tracks without the permission of the Zappa Family Trust.
57. **The Eye of Wendor** by *Mandalaband*. Featuring members of *The Moody Blues, Barclay James Harvest, 10cc* and *Steeleye*

Span, Davy Rohl's *Mandalaband* released the first of what was to be a Tolkien-esque fantasy/sword and sorcery concept album trilogy on the exploits of Florian against the evil Queen Silesandre, but unfortunately only the first volume, **The Eye of Wendor: Prophesies**, was recorded and released before the rest of the project was cancelled.

58. **Honoho** by *Pink Floyd*. One assumes that this is the name for **Wish You Were Here**, which was at #5 for *Cashbox*'s own album charts, and also at #11 on the UK charts, #4 in the Australian charts and #3 on the Italian charts that same week. (**Profondo Rosso** by *Goblin* was #6 that week in Italy).

59. #156 for two weeks on November 26th 1977 and December 3rd 1977.

60. Yugoslavia (as it then was).

61. **Dødens Triumf** by *Savage Rose*. The album had been released in 1972.

62. 33.33%. In addition to Kevin Ayers holding down the #1 and (in part) the #3 spots on the Belgian charts with **The Confessions of Dr. Dream and Other Stories** and **June 1, 1974**, respectively, *Emerson, Lake & Palmer* held the #12 position with **Welcome Back My Friends to the Show That Never Ends** live album while perhaps more interestingly, Robert Wyatt was at #14 with **Rock Bottom** and Peter Hammill was at #6 with **In Camera**.

63. Punk — 3 albums (**Moving Targets** by *Penetration* entering the charts that week at #22, **Love Bites** by *The Buzzcocks* at #29, **New Boots and Panties** by Ian Dury at #33, and we are being a bit charitable by calling the last one punk). Progressive Rock — 10 albums (or 1/6th) of the Top 60. **War of the Worlds** by Jeff Wayne (#5), **Out of the Blue** by *ELO* at #15, **Tomato** by *Yes* (#16), **Bursting Out** by *Jethro Tull* (#17), **A New World Record** by *ELO* (#50), **XII** by *Barclay James Harvest* (#53), **The Kick Inside** by Kate Bush (#54), **Dark Side of the Moon** by *Pink Floyd* (#55), **25 Years On** by *Hawklords* (#58) and **No**

Smoke Without Fire by *Wishbone Ash* (#60). This does not include releases from *10cc* or Bryan Ferry (if some feel the inclusion of *ELO* releases is somewhat chartable, I would point to the similarly charitable inclusion of the Ian Dury album as a punk album). This is not necessarily to suggest that progressive rock was still more popular than punk at this time (even though the album charts do suggest that given that there are four albums which make the Top 20, with no punk albums that high up), but it certainly paints a different picture than the historians would have us believe that progressive rock's popularity had been killed by punk. What's mainly notable is that few of the progressive rock entries are from new bands or artists, which suggests that the record industry was helping to suppress/turn their backs on new progressive rock artists (something that would change during the new wave era with the success of the "neo-prog" artists like *Marillion*).

64. **Alturas de Macchu Picchu**, the 1981 album from legendary Chilean band *Los Jaivas*.

65. *Saga*, with 18 (if you were assuming *Rush*, they "only" have had half the number that *Saga* have had, with nine studio albums charting in Germany — a run which didn't start until 1984's **Grace Under Pressure**, which peaked at #43 that year.

66. All of these progressive rock albums were produced by David Hitchcock.

67. *Jethro Tull*. Their 2022 album **The Zealot Gene** hit #9 in the UK album charts, making it their first Top 10 album there since **Thick as a Brick** in 1972. The Top 10 gap in the US was "only" 45 years, as — according to the band's own Facebook post on February 11th, 2022 — **The Zealot Gene** also hit #10 on the US Album Charts, the first time hitting the Top 10 there since **Songs From the Wood** hit #8 for three weeks in 1977.

68. **Piktors Verwandlungen** the 1981 album by *Anyone's Daughter*. The title translates as "Piktor's Transformations."

69. **Operation**, the second album by *Birth Control*. The UK album artwork depicted two huge condoms. Ironically the original German album release artwork also caused controversy as the gatefold cover depicted a monster eating babies as well as an illustration of the Pope.

70. **Bury My Heart at Wounded Knee** by the German band *Gila*. The non-fiction work of the same name by author Dee Brown had been released in 1970, three years before the album was released. *Gila* included within its ranks Florian Fricke, also a member of the German electronic progressive band *Popol Vuh* who perhaps are best known for producing the music for German director Werner Herzog films such as *Nosferatu*.

71. The progressive rock super-group *Transatlantic* with three different versions of **The Absolute Universe**. This included a 64-minute abridged version entitled **The Breath of Life**, a 90-minute single CD version entitled **Forevermore** and a 96-minute version on 2 CDs which combines parts of both the abridged and extended versions, and, just to confuse matters, also includes alternate versions of the tracks including some which have different lyrics and different band members singing on the different tracks.

72. *Pendragon*, which re-released their 2008 album **Pure** on CD in 2011 with a DVD entitled "Hand-cam Progumentary" and then also released their new 2011 album **Passion** on CD which also came with a "Progumentary" DVD.

73. They both feature tracks that reference the Silver Surfer. The only album by *Icarus* was the 1972 album **The Marvel World of Icarus** which was a concept album where every track was about a Marvel character (legend has it that the album was quickly withdrawn after a dispute between Marvel and the record company, Pye), including one track on "The Silver Surfer." The Silver Surfer is then referenced in the lyrics to the closing track on CD 1 of *Van Der Graaf Generator*'s comeback album **Present**, with the final lyric to "On The Beach" being "Even the Silver Surfer agrees..." It is a shame that the *Icarus* album didn't include a track on Dr.

Strange (Spider-Man, Hulk, Thor, Black Panther, the Fantastic Four, Captain America, Madame Masque, and even Conan the Barbarian are among the others represented on the album), as Peter Hammill also references him in the track "Time for a Change" on his **ph7** solo album from 1979.

74. **Pepper's Ghost** by *Arena*. Released in 2005, the album has something in common with *Jethro Tull's* **Too Old to Rock and Roll: Too Young to Die** in that it includes within the album artwork a comic strip depicting the events featured in the tracks included on the album.

75. They are not just self-titled albums which are not debut albums (as most self-titled albums are), but they are both self-titled albums which happen to be the 12th studio album released by each progressive band in question.

76. 22. Not bad, considering the album appears to have peaked at #59 in the chart.

77. *Happy the Man*. Gabriel apparently flew to Washington and hung out with the band and rehearsed with them for the better part of a week, just prior to the band signing with Arista Records.

78. *Anathema* with their 2nd album to make the UK Top 40, **The Optimist**.

79. **Sombra y luz,** the third album from Spanish progressive rock legends *Triana*.

80. **666** by the Greek progressive rock band *Aphrodite's Child*. The album was finally released in 1972, over a year after it was recorded, with the record company, Mercury, initially refusing to release it before relenting and putting it out on their "progressive" record label Vertigo.

Chapter Twelve — The Albums

Chapter Thirteen — The Tracks

1. "Level Five" from the 2003 album **The Power to Believe**.
2. Kate Bush. The record company had originally chosen "James and the Cold Gun" as her first single, but the teenage Bush's tears made the record executive cave in to her demand for "Wuthering Heights," which eventually went to #1 on the charts in the UK.
3. Manfred Mann.
4. "Religious Experience (Singing a Song in the Morning)."
5. Bonnie Franklin, stage and screen star (best known for playing Ann Romano on *One Day at a Time*) was reportedly the object of the obsession of a fan referenced in the lyrics to *Supertramp*'s song "Bonnie" from **Famous Last Words**.
6. Narcissus and Goldmund by Herman Hesse.
7. "Sally Don't Change It," from the album **Back to Front**.
8. Peter Sutcliffe, the Yorkshire Ripper, rather than the far more famous (but never properly identified) Jack the Ripper.
9. "Jerusalem" by *Emerson, Lake & Palmer* off **Brain Salad Surgery** in 1973.
10. "Take a Bow," the opening track from **Black Holes and Revelations**.

11. Kevin Ayers, who did the vocals for the track. Oldfield had been a member of Ayers' band *The Whole Wide World* and had played on his second and third solo albums.

12. "Ganton 9" — this was the planet that Keith Emerson originally envisaged the events of the track taking place on.

13. "Ukraine Ways" off their 1981 album **Camera Camera**. It was changed because lyric writer Betty Thatcher pointed out that the song title could be misinterpreted as "Rows of China" (presumably when heard by anyone without access to the album to see what the title of the track actually was).

14. "Das Schaffst Das Nicht" by *Grobschnitt*, a title which apparently means "You won't make it" — making one ponder how positive and uplifting the German version of *Sesame Street* is.

15. "Spoon," which was later included on the **Ege Bamyasi** album released in 1972.

16. *Renaissance*'s lead singer Annie Haslam and *ELO*'s bass player Roy Wood. The two were engaged for four years, with Wood also having produced and played on Haslam's solo album **Annie in Wonderland**.

17. Mary Whitehouse, the self-proclaimed guardian of moral values in the UK.

18. *Divodorum*. If you think that's a bad pun on my part, the joke was used in the English language version of *Asterix and the Golden Sickle* in 1975 when Obelix (trying to shake information out of someone who tells him that his friend has been taken to Divodorum) says "I don't care if you've ordered rum or not!"

19. Mike Oldfield, with "Moonlight Shadow."

20. Italy.

21. "Severity Town" by *Grobschnitt* from the concept album **Rockpommel's Land.** And no, it's not quite what you think.

22. "Red Shift" from the album **The Silent Corner and the Empty Stage**.

23. "Urban Guerilla" by *Hawkwind*.
24. Victoria Day.
25. Alan Parsons.
26. "Biko" by Peter Gabriel.
27. The band's keyboard player Woolly Wolstenholme.
28. "On My Way Home" on the album **To the Power of Three** by the Emerson-Palmer-Berry band *3*.
29. Drummer Nick Mason.
30. Kevin Ayers.
31. Rick Wakeman. It was written by David Cousins about this disappointment of Rick Wakeman leaving the band to join *Yes*.
32. Alan Parsons, who played something called the "Jaws Harp" on the track "Lady Loves" off the *BJH* album **Once Again**, released in 1971.
33. "Aqualung." Barre, we assume not seriously, suggests that the half-second break in the guitar solo to that song was the result of him very rapidly waving back to Page as he visited the band who were recording **Aqualung** in the same studio that *Led Zeppelin* were recording **Led Zeppelin IV**.
34. **Iron Maiden**.
35. Sweden and Norway, the track being "Bobby Brown."
36. "Another Frontier" — it was originally earmarked for a Keith Emerson solo album.
37. The poem *Under Milk Wood* by Dylan Thomas.
38. "Locomotive Breath," which was released as a single that year (presumably in support of the **M.U. — The Best of Jethro Tull** collection that had been released as an album that year).
39. "Mirror for the Day" by *Caravan*. Singer and writer Pye Hastings had the lyrics on a music stand in front of him when the band played the Theatre Royal on Drury Lane, a concert which would

Chapter Thirteen — The Tracks   Questions? Answers!

be released as **Caravan & The New Symphonia,** the band's only release of 1974 and their only live album released during their classic era.

40. *The Moody Blues*. This is according to Mike Pinder on *The Moody Blues* DVD documentary released in the "Classic Artists" series.

41. "Rangers at Midnight" from the album **Animal Notes** by *Crack the Sky*.

42. "Wintertell" was dropped from the album because it was allegedly "too personal" to vocalist Peter Nicholls and was not "representative" of the full band — but it was also dropped in order to make room for the track "My Baby Treats Me Right Because I'm a Hard Loving Man All Night Long" — which is a piano solo, on which only keyboardist Martin Orford and no other band members play.

43. "Shock the Monkey," Peter Gabriel's first Top 30 hit on the US Singles chart. Hammill provided backing vocals. He would later do the same for Gabriel's hit single "Digging in the Dirt" in 1992.

44. "Blue Guitar" by Justine Hayward. Subsequent CD releases of the Justine Hayward-John Lodge album **Blue Jays** (released in 1975 during the "hiatus" period for *The Moody Blues*) include this song as a bonus track on the album.

45. Three weeks. This is the claim that one of the band members makes to the audience after they provide a live version of the acapella track to the band which can be heard on the **Missing Pieces** CD compilation.

46. "Gamma Ray" by *Birth Control*, off the album **Hoodoo Man**, released in 1972.

47. "Roxane" — not the more famous song by *The Police* but the second track on side two of the concept album **Iskander** by Dutch band *Supersister*, which is a concept album about Alexander the Great.

48. "Oh! Wot a Dream" by Kevin Ayers, released as a single in 1973 and taken from his 1973 LP **Bananamour.**

49. "Going Nowhere" off their 1983 album **The Present.** Speaking to Terry David Mulligan on Canada's *Much Music* channel, Hayward recalled that it took several weeks to record this track, far longer than they normally took, because they could not get the drum parts recorded properly.

50. The 18-minute title track to *Gryphon*'s 1974 release **Midnight Mushrumps**.

Chapter Fourteen — The Lyrics

1. "The Canterbury Sequence" by *The Tangent*.
2. *No Name* (who are from Luxembourg) from their song "Downpour, Sunflowers and Sadness."
3. *RPWL*, from the track "This is Not a Prog Song" off their 2008 album **The RPWL Experience**.
4. Robert Wyatt, on the self-titled track from the album **Dondestan**.
5. William Shatner, for his progressive rock album **Ponder the Mystery** (with music written by Billy Sherwood of *Yes* fame with lead guitar on the track played by Steve Vai).
6. *Star People* (the lyrics are from the track "Kronos" from their album **Genius)**.
7. "The Sun in My Eyes" by *The Tangent*.
8. "Waterloo Lily" according to *Caravan* from their 1972 album of the same name.
9. "le réveil/the dawn" by *Eloy* from the 1976 album **Dawn**. And no, not from an earlier version of a certain *Yes* song off **Tales from Topographic Oceans**.

10. *Squackett*, the band formed by Chris Squire and Steve Hackett from their sole LP, 2012's **A Life Within a Day**.

11. *Novalis*, from their 1975 self-titled album (which was not their first release incidentally). The track in question that the lyrics are taken from is "Wer Schmetterlinge Lachen Hört."

12. "Ooby-Scooby Doomsday or The D-Day DJ's Got the DDT Blues" by *Gong*.

13. "Let's Eat (Real Soon)" by *Hatfield and the North*.

14. *The Tangent* from the track "Codpieces and Capes."

15. "Seven is a Jolly Good Time" by *Egg*, a song that extols the virtues of playing in seven-time rather than four.

16. "Soft Royce" from the Dutch progressive rock band *Alquin*. Appropriately, the track (and band in general) sound a bit like a cross between *Chicago* and the *Soft Machine*.

17. "A.A. Man" by *Caravan*. Written by Richard Sinclair, the A.A. Man referenced is the UK's Automobile Association men who help with car breakdowns.

18. "Kismet in Suburbia" from **Thick as a Brick 2** by *Jethro Tull's Ian Anderson*.

19. "Zabaglione," a track which (sans lyrics) can be heard on *National Health*'s **Missing Pieces** CD release featuring (mostly) previously unreleased tracks.

20. "Vegetable Man" by *Pink Floyd*, one of the last tracks written by Syd Barrett that the band recorded, which did not get an official release until 2016. Why is there a look of non-surprise on your face as you read this?

21. Geddy Lee of *Rush* on "Tears Are Not Enough," a single released by **Northern Lights for Africa**, Canada's contribution (also featuring the likes of Neil Young, Gordon Lightfoot, Joni Mitchell, Bruce Cockburn, and Burton Cummings of *The Guess Who*) to the wave of charity singles that came in the wake of the Ethiopian

famine first drawn attention to, musically speaking, by *Band-Aid*'s "Do They Know It's Christmas" single.

22. *Ambrosia* for the song "Nice, Nice, Very Nice," which reached #63 on the hit parade in 1975 in the US (and also got significant airplay in Canada).

23. "Automation Horrorscope" by *Nektar*.

24. The British progressive rock band *Home* with the opening lyrics to "Red E. Lewis and the Red Caps" from their debut album from 1971, **Pause for a Hoarse Horse**. The band's next album just missed the top 40 in the US hitting #41 while their third and last was released in 1973, entitled **The Alchemist**. The bass player for the band was Cliff Williams who played with *AC/DC* for nearly 40 years starting in 1977. Lead singer and guitarist Mick Stubbs played with Jimmy Page in the band referred to in the song title in pre-*Yardbirds* days.

25. The lyrics to all three refer either directly or allegorically to *The Beatles*.

26. "My Legs" by *IQ*. The quote of the description of the track is taken from the CD release **The Lost Attic — A Collection of Rarities 1983–1999** on which the track is included.

27. *Matching Mole*, the band Robert Wyatt formed after leaving (or being pushed out of) the *Soft Machine*. The track in question is "O Caroline."

28. Specifically, Peter Blevgad with a spoken word extract used on the track "Squarer for Maud" by *National Health*.

29. "5.5.55" by German band *Amon Duul II* from their concept album detailing German history from the late 19th century through to WWII.

30. "Corporation Combo Boys" off the album **Present From Nancy**, the debut album by Dutch Canterbury-style band *Supersister*.

31. *Styx*. The lyrics belong to the John Curulewski-penned track "As Bad As This," which can be found on the band's third LP, **The Serpent is Rising**.
32. "The Pin Drop" by Steven Wilson off his solo album from 2013, **The Raven Who Refused to Sing and Other Stories**.
33. Specifically, Tom Baker who was the 4th Doctor in *Doctor Who*. However, he didn't say that in *Doctor Who* but on the 2020 album from *Ayreon*, **Transitus**, for which he is the spoken-word narrator for the album. Baker was chosen as he is the favourite Doctor of Arjen Anthony Lucassen (who effectively is *Ayreon*).
34. **In Amazonia**, a 2019 album released by Peter Hammill and the Swedish progressive rock band *Isildur's Bane*, in which the music was written and performed by the *Isildur's Bane* while the lyrics are written and sung by Peter Hammill.
35. "The White Rider" by *Camel* off their 1974 album **Mirage**. The lyrics describe the incident which sees "Gandalf the Grey" become "Gandalf the White."

Chapter Fifteen — The Concerts

1. *Watcher of the Skies.* Hackett had the audience for a solo show he performed in Massey Hall in 2018 recite these words when performing a "Genesis Revisited" show there decades later.
2. *IQ.*
3. *Hawkwind.*
4. Montreal.
5. London, Ontario.
6. *Kraan.*
7. Christian Vander of *Magma*. Vander responded with a derisive "Yeah, whatever buddy." The author of this book witnessed these events for himself.
8. *Camel, Colosseum II, Gentle Giant, Jethro Tull, Procol Harum, Renaissance, The Strawbs, Supertramp.* Gordon Giltrap, and *Be Bop Deluxe* (who are often considered "Prog-related," if not actually Prog, also featured). *Marillion* would appear in the 1983–1984 season of this show.
9. *Yes.*
10. Buffalo, New York.
11. *Van Der Graaf Generator.*
12. *Iron Maiden* (specifically, bassist/founder Steve Harris and drummer Nicko McBain).

Chapter Fifteen — The Concerts   Questions? Answers!

13. *Family.*
14. *Camel.*
15. Rick Wakeman.
16. Ian Anderson of *Jethro Tull*. There are unconfirmed reports of him doing this as early as the 1972 Thick as a Brick tour on the Toronto show at Maple Leaf Gardens, but it was regularly done on the **Songs from the Wood** tour of 1977. He began by playing the acoustic number "Wondering Aloud," before being joined by the other members of the band who had been shrouded in darkness.
17. *Henry Cow* (England), *Stormy Six* (Italy), *Univers Zero* (Belgium), *Samla Mammas Manna* (Sweden) and *Etron Fou Leloublan* (France).
18. *U.K.*
19. 7. *Kansas* was responsible for three of the entries (including being supported by *Starcastle* in front of over 21,000 fans in St. Louis), *Emerson, Lake & Palmer* (touring Florida) provided two other entries and *Jethro Tull* (touring further up the country playing dates in Kentucky and North Carolina) provided the final two.
20. *Yes* on their tour for **Relayer** and apparently 48 hours later, *Genesis* on their **Lamb Lies Down on Broadway** tour.
21. Pete Sinfield, promoting his solo album *Still* (released again decades later on CD with two new tracks and a revised track order as *Stillusion*).
22. *Grobschnitt.*
23. Jean-Michel Jarre.
24. Todd Rundgren's band *Nazz*.
25. *Barclay James Harvest.*
26. *Saga.* The Caribbean Island in question was Puerto Rico.
27. Tim Blake, formerly of *Gong*.

Questions? Answers!   Chapter Fifteen — The Concerts

28. *Magma* and *Ange*.
29. *Novalis*
30. *Van Der Graaf* (as *Van Der Graaf Generator* were then known). The band would of course reform and start to play concerts again 27 years later in 2005.
31. *Jethro Tull* at Madison Square Gardens in October 1978. *Uriah Heep* opened the show.
32. *Pink Floyd*. 55,000 people showed up at the stadium that is built in a residential area in downtown Hamilton, which meant that most residents living near the stadium got little sleep that night.
33. Japan.
34. The Beacon Theatre in New York. This is the same number of concerts that they played in Rimouski, Quebec that decade.
35. *Rush* and *Starcastle* who performed on a triple-bill with *Boston* at the Riverfront Colosseum in Cincinnati, Ohio on March 4th 1977. Another *Boston/Starcastle* gig (without *Rush*) held in Madison Wisconsin that week was at #6.
36. *Genesis*.
37. It was the last concert *Gentle Giant* ever played in their homeland of the UK.
38. *Jethro Tull* and *Yes*, with a little help from *Uriah Heep*. Although a Steve Martin live comedy performance topped the box office charts that week, in terms of music two *Jethro Tull* concerts (supported by *Uriah Heep*) led the box office charts, while *Yes* were responsible for three of the next four entries on the chart (with only a Bob Dylan concert coming in after the first & second *Yes* concerts that week breaking up the complete Prog dominance of the concert charts that particular week).
39. Pablo Picasso.
40. At the Plymouth Guildhall in front of 3000 fans. Contrary to urban legend and despite what MC Rikki Farr says at the Isle of Wight

Concert at the end of August 1970, *ELP*'s concert at the Isle of Wight Festival was not their "first-ever debut performance," it occurred just before that in Plymouth.

Chapter Sixteen — Plaudits and Pundits

1. Alan Jones. His review of *Dark Side of the Moon* described the album as a "vacuum." It's a good thing that the record buyers paid attention to his recommendations stayed away from purchasing these two albums in their droves, isn't it?

2. Lester Bangs.

3. *Jethro Tull* for the video to their 1989 track "Kissing Willie."

4. "Land of Confusion."

5. "Cinema" by *Yes* and "Marooned" by *Pink Floyd*.

6. Vangelis, who won the award in March 1982 for "Best Original Music Score" for *Chariots of Fire*, which was released in 1981.

7. Simon Frith. Edward Macan takes Frith's claim to task in his excellent book *Rocking the Classics: English Progressive Rock and the Counterculture.*

8. Creem.

9. *Saga* won the award in 1982, even though they had three albums released before 1981, one of which (1980's **Silent Knight)** charted high enough in Canada to reach the Top 50. Despite this (and the fact that the band had already had hit singles and received radio airplay for their earlier albums), the band got the de facto "Best New Group" award for their 1981 success in **Worlds**

Apart. (*Rush* has previously won this award, but did so in March 1975 on the basis of their first album which had been released in 1974 — in other words, they won when they were actually still a new group). Incidentally, one of the bands *Saga* beat out was Tom Cochrane's band *Red Rider* — which somehow also had been nominated for the same award the previous year.

10. The band who won, *Myles and Lenny,* didn't release any more music after 1975. By comparison, *Maneige* continued to regularly produce new albums into the early 1980s. Incidentally, another one of the nominated bands who didn't win was *Heart,* who, at that time, was considered and qualified as a Canadian band as all of the members of the band, although American, had relocated to Canada in the early 70s because of the desire of the male members to avoid being sent to Vietnam. Arguably, *Heart* not winning the award is more ridiculous than *Maneige* if you judge the award on the basis of the "promising" part relating to longevity and sustained commercial success.

11. *The Enid.* There is no record indicating which group won the award for "Band Least Likely to Succeed" that year.

12. Nash the Slash.

13. *Novalis.* Ironically, rumour has it that the members of the band *Novalis* said the exact same thing about the review printed in *Musik Express.*

14. Richard Williams of *Melody Maker* in a review of **In the Wake of Poseidon** from 1970. Incidentally, the Wagner he is referring to was not Robert Wagner, especially since he was alive in 1970 and doesn't particularly have anything to do with music.

15. *Henry Cow.*

16. *Camel.* There is also no record of which band won "Dimmest Hope," in case anyone is wondering.

17. *Styx.*

18. A Trick of the Tail by *Genesis.*

19. Alan Parsons, who at that time, rarely did any singing.

20. **Four Moments** by Australian progressive rock band *Sebastian Hardie*.

21. The self-titled debut album from Pittsburgh-based band, *Crack the Sky*. Despite the plaudits, the album only reached 161 in the US Billboard album charts.

22. "Don't Give Up" by Peter Gabriel, which features a vocal duet with Kate Bush. The award was given in 1987.

23. *Porcupine Tree*'s **Fear of a Blank Planet**, released in 2007. Fripp is not a member of Steven Wilson's band but he provided "soundscapes" for the track "Way Out of Here." Alex Lifeson of *Rush* also appears on this album, playing guitar on the track "Anesthetize."

24. **Yeti**, the double-LP by German band *Amon Duul II*.

25. *Focus* (in 1973) and *Earth and Fire* (in 1980). The award is handed out in the Netherlands to the Dutch artist that sells the most records abroad in a given year. *Focus* won it in just the second year of the Award's existence.

Chapter Sixteen — Plaudits and Pundits

Chapter Seventeen — Progressive Rock at the Cinema

1. **Foxtrot** by *Genesis*.
2. Soft Machine's **Third**.
3. *Buffalo 66*. The movie also featured topless dancers dancing in slow motion while "Heart of the Sunrise" by *Yes* is played, while the closing credits features "Sweetness," also by *Yes*.
4. *Almost Famous*.
5. 1982.
6. Peter Baumann.
7. Weird Science.
8. *I Love You, Man*. The band performs "Limelight" from the 1981 album **Moving Pictures**.
9. *Big Daddy*. The irony is that *Jethro Tull* never actually broke up (or by the time that this film was released in 1999) or had stopped touring, so it wasn't actually possible for the band to have played a "reunion" concert, unless he was somehow referring to the original band members reuniting with Ian Anderson. Chances are

though that the filmmakers were aware of the band's massive popularity in the 1970s and assumed that they had ceased to function sometime before the film was made.

10. *X, Y and Zee* (1972) — the members in question are Rick Wakeman and Dave Lambert.

11. *Images* (1972).

12. Goblin for *Suspiria* (1977), Keith Emerson for *Inferno* (1980) and Claudio Simonetti (former member of *Goblin*) for *Mother of Tears* (2007), a trilogy of films directed by Dario Argento. Thom Yorke of *Radiohead* would provide the soundtrack for a 2018 remake of *Suspiria*.

13. *Yes*.

14. George "Zoot" Money, whom the character of "Zoot" from *Monty Python and the Holy Grail* is named after.

15. Rick Wakeman and Justin Hayward.

16. **Tales of Mystery and Imagination (Edgar Allen Poe)** by *The Alan Parsons Project* and **Jeff Wayne's Musical Version of War of the Worlds.** Orson Welles (who did the narration for the former) and Richard Burton (who did the narration for the latter) both star in this film, alongside Elizabeth Taylor.

17. A Dalek from *Doctor Who*. John Scott Martin was one of the original Daleks in 1963 and still played them in their last appearance in the classic series in 1988.

18. *The Children of Men*.

19. *Pink Floyd* and Ian Anderson of *Jethro Tull*. Tull's label, *Chrysalis Records* and *Charisma Records*, the label owned by Tony Stratton-Smith who was the manager for such progressive rock bands as *The Nice*, *Genesis* and *Van Der Graaf Generator* (whose albums were released on that label) also contributed finances. Idle released the information in a Tweet in 2020.

20. Roger Waters, for "Another Brick in the Wall," which of course was written for a 1979 studio album and then used in a film. The

award was discontinued after Ray Parker Jr. won it in 1985 for "Ghostbusters." Whether this was because of the embarrassment that this "original" song was sued for plagiarism by Huey Lewis of *Huey Lewis and the News* is unknown.

21. Vangelis. Two years before he had done the score for another 80s sci-fi classic, *Blade Runner*.
22. Rick Wakeman. The film was called *G'olé!*
23. Roger Dean (we meant artist is the traditional painting/artwork sense — sorry!). Dean was referring to his books containing his sci-fi/fantasy imagery that also included countless progressive rock covers and interior artwork.
24. "Nights in White Satin" by *The Moody Blues*.
25. **Rime of the Ancient Mariner** by David Bedford and **Journey to the Centre of the Earth** by Rick Wakeman. The respective narrators of these two albums (Robert Powell and David Hemmings) collaborated on *The Survivor*, with Powell starring and Hemmings directing the film.
26. *Pavlov's Dog*. The track in question is "Of Once and Future Kings," from their debut album, 1976's **Pampered Menial**.
27. **Attahk** by *Magma*.
28. *Pink Floyd* and *Magma* were lined up to do the music. *Gong*, *Tangerine Dream* and *Mike Oldfield* had previously been approached.
29. *Simon Dupree* and the Big Sound who later became *Gentle Giant*.
30. Dave Lawson, vocalist and one of the keyboardists for *Greenslade*.
31. "New York Girls" on the 1975 album **Commoner's Crown** by *Steeleye Span*.
32. "Roundabout" by *Yes*.
33. John Barleycorn Must Die by *Traffic*.

Chapter Seventeen — Progressive Rock at the Cinema   Questions? Answers!

34. *Jethro Tull's* **Thick as a Brick** and **A Passion Play**. In the latter album, Derek Small is the name given to a character played by *Jethro Tull* guitarist Martin Barre.

35. Mick Shrimpton, the drummer who spontaneously combusts on stage, was played by R.J. Parnell who can count *Atomic Rooster* and Italian bands *Ibis* and *Nova* as past progressive rock bands that he played with.

36. *Ambrosia*.

37. *The Devil's Triangle* from 1974, which, as one might guess, features *King Crimson's* track of the same name in the soundtrack.

38. "Lark's Tongues in Aspic — Part Two" was used in *Emmanuelle*, also released in 1974.

39. Manfred Mann, who appears as a jazz pianist in the legendary Spanish director's 1969 film *Venus in Furs*.

40. *Death Wish II*. The soundtrack to the sequel to the Charles Bronson film of 1974 was written by Jimmy Page who also played guitar on it. Dave Lawson of *Greenslade* was the keyboardist, David Paton (who sang on both 1982's **The Single Factor** and 1984's **Stationary Traveller** (from *Camel*)) played bass while one-time *Jethro Tull* drummer (on the **A Little Light Music** live album from 1992) David Mattacks did percussion.

41. *Ladyhawke*. The soundtrack for the film would eventually be done by Andrew Powell (who often collaborated with *The Alan Parsons Project*) and would be produced by Alan Parsons himself.

42. **That's What You Get Babe** by Kevin Ayers, released 1980. Zimmer played the starlight synthesizer on the album.

43. "Dirk" Mont Campbell of *Egg* and *National Health*. Mont Campbell was the grandson of renowned British composer Martin Shaw, whose nephew (and thus a cousin of Campbell) was Sebastien Shaw, who played the unmasked Darth Vader in *Return of the Jedi*.

116

Questions? Answers! Chapter Seventeen — Progressive Rock at the Cinema

44. All five of these albums can be seen displayed in the "Championship Vinyl" record store in the 2000 John Cusack film *High Fidelity*.

45. John Williams, the Australian classical guitarist (not the composer John Williams famed for *Star Wars, Indiana Jones, Jaws* etc.) who was a member of the classical rock band *Sky* from 1979 to 1984. William's recording of *Cavatina* was originally used for the 1970 film *The Walking Stick* but became much more famous when re-used for the 1978 Best Picture Oscar-winning film *The Deer Hunter*. Released as a single it made the UK Top 20.

46. *Harmonium*. The Quebec-based band led by Serge Fiori (who can be seen in the film humorously advising the American audience that the band only sings in French), was conducting their first concert performances in the United States. The film was entitled *Harmonium en Californie* and released in October 1979.

47. Arthur Brown, who was only a couple of years away finding fame with his hit song "Fire" released by his band *The Crazy World of Arthur Brown*. The film, released in the US as *The Game is Over*, was directed by Roger Vadim who was married to Jane Fonda at this time, and would later direct her in *Barbarella*.

48. "Dust in the Wind" by *Kansas* in the film *Old School* (2003) and "Aqualung" by *Jethro Tull* in the film *Anchorman: The Legend of Ron Burgundy*.

49. The Adam Sandler film *That's My Boy* (2012) and the Will Ferrell film *Anchorman II — The Legend Continues* (2013).

50. Iron Man himself, Robert Downey Jr., covered the "Your Move" part of *Yes*'s "I've Seen All Good People" on his 2004 album *The Futurist*, with Jon Anderson's vocals featured in the background. Zappa-alumni drummer Vinnie Colaiuta (whose name is immortalized in the Zappa song "Catholic Girls" from **Joe's Garage**) also plays on this album.

Chapter Seventeen — Progressive Rock at the Cinema   Questions? Answers!

Chapter Eighteen — Progressive Rock on Television

1. *King Crimson*'s **In the Wake of Poseidon** — in particular, the track "The Devil's Triangle."
2. Thick as a Brick by *Jethro Tull*.
3. *Emerson, Lake & Palmer*.
4. **Stand Up**.
5. *Life on Mars*
6. "Black Sand" from the album **Cottonwoodhill**.
7. Adam Dalgliesh, based on the novels written by P.D. James.
8. *Blake's Seven*.
9. Edwin Drood.
10. Douglas Adams.
11. *Greenslade*.
12. "Colony in Space."
13. "You by My Side" by Chris Squire from his 1975 solo album **Fish out of Water**.

14. *The Prisoner* — specifically, the "Rover" balloon device that was used to capture escaping prisoners from the Village.
15. "Tintagel by the Sea."
16. "Back Home Once Again" by *Renaissance*.
17. "Tubular Bells" by *Mike Oldfield*.
18. The plaintiff was Patrick Moraz, who was suing the four then-current members of *The Moody Blues* for lost earnings after they had fired him from the band. Central to the dispute was whether Moraz had been a full member of the band or a guest/session musician.
19. "Spoon" by *Can*.
20. *Family*.
21. "The Rime of the Ancient Mariner" by David Bedford.
22. "Stanley Stump's Gibbon Album" by the *Soft Machine* off the 1973 album "Six."
23. *Twelfth Night*
24. Robin Lumley of *Brand X*.
25. "House of the King" by *Focus*.
26. "Cup of Wonder" and "Acres Wild."
27. Another Brick in the Wall (Part 2) by *Pink Floyd*.
28. *Star Cops*.
29. Trudy Young. The Canadian actress, perhaps most famous for playing a hippy rock singer in the 1971 Canadian film *Face-off*, was the voice of the groupie on the track "One of My Turns" on *Pink Floyd*'s **The Wall**.
30. Phil Manzanera. The *Roxy Music* and *Quiet Sun* guitarist's hands pretend to be that of the Psiren version of Dave Lister in the Series Six episode "Psirens."

31. *Caravan.* The pre-recorded video performance was of the track "Heartbreaker," the broadcast of which was interrupted on May 13th, 1981.
32. Kate Bush. The episode in question was the story "Human Nature," originally written by Paul Cornell as a novel before being adapted for television.
33. *Pink Floyd.* There is no word on whether their music was considered more or less bizarre than *The Soft Machine's*.
34. *Blake's Seven.* "Star One" is the name of the final episode of the series' 2nd season and is the focus of much of that season's story arc.
35. Tristam Cary.
36. Carl Sagan's Cosmos: A Personal Journey.
37. *The Nice, Santana* and *Jethro Tull.*
38. **Caught Five Plus Live.** The artist in question also did the portrait of Jon Anderson that can be found among the inner sleeve artwork for **Olias of Sunhillow**. His *Doctor Who* Target novelization covers include *The Mutants, The Face of Evil, The Talons of Weng-Chiang, The Tomb of the Cybermen, The Time Meddler, The Giant Robot, The Doomsday Weapon* and *The Dinosaur Invasion.*
39. Regis Philbin and Kathy Lee Gifford.
40. Script for a Jester's Tear by *Marillion.*
41. **The Rotter's Club** by *Hatfield and the North*. Actors (and *Doctor Who* fans) David Tennant and Frank Skinner starred in the Radio play.
42. "Phasing" by German Prog band *Hoelderlin* from the album **Clowns & Clouds.**
43. *Seventh Wave* (the composer in question was keyboard player Ken Elliott).
44. *Druid,* who were produced by Bob Harris.

45. Ian Anderson of *Jethro Tull*.

46. *Life on Mars*. "I Had a Dream" was included on the Soundtrack CD for the series, but the *Barclay James Harvest* tune (along with a ton of other early 70s music) was left off it.

47. They are the tracks that Frank Zappa played the two times he appeared on *Saturday Night Live* before he was banned from the show for reasons to do with Frank's non-conformity (to either the scripts written for him to say or for his strong anti-drug stance, depending upon who you believe).

48. *Supernatural*.

49. *Bi Kyo Ran*, often dubbed the "Japanese King Crimson."

50. *Birth Control*. The drummer in question was Egon Balder, who had been replaced by drummer, vocalist, and primary band member Bernd Noske by the time the band released their self-titled debut album in 1970.

Chapter Nineteen — Quotes

1. Rick Wakeman.

2. Former manager of *Jethro Tull* Terry Ellis, then still head of their record label, Chrysalis Records, upon hearing their 1984 album **Under Wraps** for the first time. According to the book *Minstrels in the Gallery — A History of Jethro Tull* by David Rees, Ellis had immediately preceded this comment with "If you think I'm going to release this fucking pile of crap on my label, you can think again!"

3. Alan Parsons, liner notes to the CD release of **I Robot**.

4. Daevid Allen.

5. Hans Bäär, bass player for *Hoelderlin*.

6. Dave Stewart, keyboardist for *National Health*, in the liner notes of the *National Health Complete* CD compilation.

7. Jon Anderson referring to his former bandmate in *Yes* Chris Squire.

8. Terry Brown, producer of all of *Rush*'s albums from 1975 through to 1982, on the liner notes of *FM*'s 2015 album **Transformation** which Brown mixed.

9. Kevin Ayers on *Soft Machine* producer Tom Wilson.

Chapter Nineteen — Quotes　　　　　　　　　　　　Questions? Answers!

10. *Rolling Stone* review from October 1970 of *Uriah Heep*'s first studio album, **...very 'eavy...very 'umble.**

11. Peter Hammill, referring to concerts held by *Van Der Graaf Generator* circa 1969.

12. Kalle Weber, drummer for German progressive hard rock band *Kin Ping Meh,* from the liner notes to the CD release of their self-titled album.

13. Mike Portnoy, drummer for *Dream Theatre* and *Transatlantic.*

14. Dave Stewart of National Health, in the liner notes of the **National Health Complete** CD compilation.

15. Dik Mik, electronics player for *Hawkwind*, liner notes for their self-titled debut album 1970.

16. Headline of the *New Music Express* article ridiculing the American journalist who started the "Are *Klaatu* really *The Beatles*?" theory/rumour.

17. "Roger Waters, discussing the 1970 *Pink Floyd* album he helped to write, perform and record in Mojo Magazine.

18. Nick Lowe, when asked about the music of Siouxsie and the Banshees.

19. John Woloschuk of *Klaatu,* lamenting that the hype generated for the band by the American press speculating that they were *The Beatles* ultimately doomed the band once it was discovered they were not — even though the band never claimed to be *The Beatles* in the first place.

20. Writer William S. Burroughs (considered one of the fathers of the "Beat Generation"), speaking to Daevid Allen. According to Allen, "The 1-minute one meant sex. The other didn't. I took the other one."

21. Ian Anderson — the quote can be found at: https://www.songfacts.com/blog/interviews/ian-anderson-of-jethro-tull

22. Renate Knaup, singer with *Amon Duul II* discussing the freedom and liberty enjoyed by those hippies dropping out of mainstream society and into communes. Eventually *Amon Duul II* formed out of the commune in question (and yes Renate was able to make music with the band).

23. Carl Palmer, speaking to Dom Lawson of Prog magazine on why writing a progressive rock album in the Bahamas (for *ELP*'s **Love Beach**) wasn't a good idea. (Although in this author's opinion, it is an excellent album, especially for listening to on vacations to the Caribbean).

24. Ian Anderson (from the same link listed above in answer #21).

25. Richard Sinclair, referring to *Caravan*'s appearance at the Kraalingen Pop Festival in Rotterdam, Holland in 1970.

26. David Pegg, apparently quoting Terry Ellis, former manager and then-current president of *Jethro Tull*'s label, *Chrysalis Records*.

27. Robert Wyatt.

28. Translation of a comment from Pablo Tofani of the Italian band *Area*, one of seemingly several billion progressive rock artists who, at one point or another, denied being seen as part of or classified as part of the progressive rock movement, despite the obvious musical similarities and affinities with the broader musical style/movement.

29. Bill Bruford, referring to the regular breaking-up that *King Crimson* would do.

30. Roger Waters, speaking in 1999 about former *Pink Floyd* bandmate David Gilmour.

31. Steve Hackett, referring to the effect *King Crimson*'s music had on the audience of the Marquee Club after one of their earliest gigs there in 1969.

32. Rick Wakeman, who added that Progressive Rock is "down to musicianship. It's down to brains to fingers, as opposed to brains to machines."

33. Gordon Haskell, referring to *King Crimson*'s early concerts at the venues such as the Speakeasy and the Marquee Club when they began in 1969. Haskell was a friend of Robert Fripp and would briefly join the band as a vocalist the following year.

34. Fish, the lead singer in the 1980s for *Marillion* discussing how the rock critics' evil plans to kill Prog might have succeeded, if it weren't for those darn kids in his band.

35. Rick Wakeman, expressing his unhappiness over the keyboard overdubs that were used on the **Union** LP by *Yes*.

36. Geddy Lee of *Rush* speaking in 1981 about some of the "new wave" bands.

37. Thijs Van Leer.

38. Kevin Ayers.

39. Roger Taylor, drummer of *Queen*.

40. Steve Hackett.

41. Gordon Haskell, speaking decades later about his former bandmate in *King Crimson*, Pete Sinfield.

42. Ray Shulman, bassist for *Gentle Giant* on the prospects of the band ever reuniting.

43. Pete Sinfield, when asked if he'd heard Ozzy Osbourne's version of *King Crimson's* "21st Century Schizoid Man."

44. The producer of *Grobschnitt*'s self-titled debut album discussing *Grobschnitt*. This led to the German band firing one of their two drummers and going with just the one drummer.

45. Cedric Bixler-Zavala of *The Mars Volta*.

46. Michael Karoli of *Can*.

47. William Shatner, referring to Rick Wakeman who played on his Christmas music album **Shatner Claus**. Wakeman had previously played on his progressive rock album, **Ponder the Mystery**.

48. Tony Banks, discussing "The Battle of Epping Forest" from **Selling England By the Pound**.

49. *Ayreon*'s Anthony Arjen Lucassen discussing film star Rutger Hauer's preparation for his narration of Lucassen's solo album **Lost in New Real**.

50. William Shatner referring to Ian Anderson of *Jethro Tull* after he contributed flute to Shatner's rendition of *Silver Bells*.

51. Kevin Ayers, describing the music that being made by his *Soft Machine* bandmates when he first met them in Canterbury.

52. Eroc (drummer for *Grobschnitt*) in relation to why he wrote the *Village People* parody song "A.C.Y.M."

53. Bill Bruford, talking about his fellow drummer at *King Crimson*, Jamie Muir.

54. Daevid Allen, speaking about Robert Wyatt.

55. Ian McDonald of *King Crimson* to Pete Sinfield before they became members of the original line-up of the band (this quote according to Pete Sinfield himself).

56. *Genesis* who placed this ad in *Melody Maker*, catching the eye of guitarist/writer Steve Hackett, leading him to join the band.

57. Jonathan Mover, former *Marillion* drummer who was the drummer for the Howe/Steve Hackett band *GTR*. He said these words to Howe as he temporarily quit the band, only to be persuaded by Hackett to change his mind.

58. Greg Lake.

59. Martin Orford, keyboard player for (appropriately enough given the comment) *IQ* from the 1980s to the 2000s.

60. Terence P. Minogue, co-producer for three of *Crack the Sky*'s first four albums. Note that he was not talking about *Crack the Sky* with this quote, but rather his role at Cashman & West auditioning bands — of which *Crack the Sky* were an exception in that they didn't suck (i.e., weren't "evil") at their audition.

61. Ian Anderson of *Jethro Tull* for the 2022 release **The Zealot Gene**, the first new studio album from the band since either 1999, 2003, or 2012 (depending on one's point of view).

62. "Mmm... Because it is time to go. I don't know. Shit happens."

Chapter Twenty — Miscellaneous

1. 1991. Seemingly still bitter about *Tull* having been awarded the Grammy for "Best Hard Rock/Heavy Metal Album" of 1987 (as well as not comprehending the simple fact that the category could include music that was considered hard rock rather than music that was exclusively heavy metal) in the 1992 Grammy Awards (for music released in 1991), *Metallica* opened their acceptance speech for thanking *Jethro Tull* for not having released an album in 1991. The irony, of course, was that *Tull* had released an album that year, **Catfish Rising**.

2. Justin Hayward and John Lodge of *The Moody Blues*. Although the proceeds of the single went to charity, the intention for the song was to raise awareness of BBC management's then-current intention to cancel the long-running science-fiction series *Doctor Who*.

3. Dame Edna (aka Barry Humphries).

4. Ian Anderson of *Jethro Tull*.

5. Blue Weaver, who had been the replacement for Rick Wakeman in *The Strawbs* after the latter had left them to join *Yes*.

6. Kate Bush. The video in question was for "Babooshka."

7. Eddie Van Halen, according to *Guitar World* magazine.

8. Derek Shulman of *Gentle Giant*. After the band broke up in 1980, he became an "A&R" man with Polygram Records where he signed the likes of *Bon Jovi* and *Cinderella*.

9. Zero. None. Nada. Nil. Zilch. While it has to be said that *The Sex Pistols* sole studio album didn't get released until November 11th of that year in North America, it remains a fact that the Top 100 selling albums in Canada in 1977 include no punk albums but as many as 11 progressive rock (or Prog Rock-related in some cases) releases (**A New World** at #3, **Even in the Quietest Moments** at #6, **Leftoverture** at #25, **A Day at the Races** at #38, **Songs from the Wood** at #41, **The Roaring Silence** #45, **Going for the One** #47, **Point of Know Return** at #59, **A Farewell to Kings** at #66, **I Robot** at #68, **Animals** at #77 and **Works — Volume One** at #100). In case any pro-punk historians or critics reading this are under the delusion that the flood of punk album sales must have flowed into 1978 following the release of **Never Mind the Bollocks, Here's the Sex Pistols** in late 1977, think again. No punk albums featured in the Top 100 selling albums in Canada in 1978 either. While it's a less successful year for progressive rock ("only" **Point of Know Return** at #10, **The Grand Illusion** at #14, **Pieces of Eight** at #29, **Out of the Blue** at #46, **A Farewell to Kings** at #65, **And Then There Were Three** at #85, **Heavy Horses** at #91, and **Life Beyond L.A.** at #97), it's not because the Prog albums were being replaced by punk artists — instead there is a surge in disco, stadium rock (Foreigner, Boston, KISS). Incidentally, **Sgt. Pepper** was #95.

10. "Think Twice" which was sung by Celine Dion to the top of the charts of 8 different nations.

11. Tim Blake (who, in addition to his own solo albums, as previously been a member of both *Gong* and *Hawkwind* and played on two *Clearlight* albums).

12. Jerney Kaagman, lead singer of hugely successful Dutch band *Earth and Fire* appeared in the Dutch edition of the magazine (at the age of 35).

13. Franco Falsini of *Sensations Fix*.
14. Carlo Karges, who had been a member of *Novalis* in 1974 and 1975, playing both guitar and keyboard.
15. *Magma*.
16. *Genesis*. It was apparently bass player Mike Rutherford's suggestion during the Peter Gabriel-era of the band.
17. Elton Dean, who was a member of *Soft Machine* for their albums **Third, Fourth** and **Fifth** (released 1970, 1971 and 1972, respectively).
18. The members of *Gentle Giant* when they were still in their pre-progressive incarnation, *Simon Dupree and the Big Sound*. Apparently Syd Barrett let the cat out of the bag as to who *The Moles* really were.
19. *Van Der Graaf Generator* in a tour of Italy in 1975. They managed to recover most of their equipment with the help of the British Embassy in Italy.
20. *Focus*. He was spotted by both guitarist Jan Akkerman and keyboard/flautist Thijs Van Leer.
21. "Echoes," which had actually been written 20 years earlier.
22. The band had been told that unless they did so, they would not receive the full publishing proceeds due to an alleged insufficient number of tracks for an album. Hence the tracks had extra titles added to them to denote additional tracks within them (e.g. "In the Court of the Crimson King" includes "The Return of the Fire Witch: and "The Dance of the Puppets" within it).
23. The Aqualung Corporation of North America. "Aqualung" was actually a registered trademarked name, which no one in *Jethro Tull* was aware of. The lawsuit was dropped however and never pursued without anyone connected to the band having to pay them a penny.
24. Ian Underwood, who played synthesizers on the track.

25. Marc Bolan of *T-Rex*, shortly before his death in a car accident.

26. Phil Collins. Of course, Phil was mainly a drummer back in 1969-70 and was auditioning for the drummer position in the jazz-rock precursor to the more famous progressive rock band (*Manfred Mann's Earth Band*) that formed in the early 70s.

27. Chris Squire. The incident (and the *Yes* reunion that the band imagined happening) is detailed in the liner notes to *The Flower Kings* DVD **"Tour Kaputt."**

28. They are three original-era progressive rock bands where there isn't a single member who can say that they played or featured in every official studio album. *Yes* joined this group when they released **The Quest** in 2021, following the passing of Chris Squire who had been the only member to have played on every previous studio album. As for *Gong*, arguably they entered this club in 1975 with **Shamal** but even if one considered that band the start of *Pierre Moerlen's Gong* (as later albums in the 1970s would be known and entitled), and even considering that Daevid Allen's vocals are posthumously included the band's first album following his passing (2016's **Rejoice! I'm Dead!**), the band released 2019's **The Universe Also Collapses** without any involvement from Allen.

29. *Rush.*

30. Not English, French, or even Kobian — but "American." Yes, I know that's not an actual language, but that's what Thibault said in the documentary on *Magma* **To Life and Death Beyond** so it must be true.

31. Berlin.

32. David Hitchcock.

33. *Camel*, who were touring **The Snow Goose** circa 1975.

34. "Too Old to Rock and Roll: Too Young to Die." Quite honestly, for the purposes of irony (as they reportedly picked tracks from many other artists for the ironic value, such as *Van Halen*'s "Panama" and Bruce Cockburn's "If I Had a Rocket Launcher"), they should

have gone with the opening track "Fly By Night" from Ian Anderson's 1983 solo album **Walk Into Light**.

35. Rick Moranis, who went to grade school with Geddy Lee. Lee would feature as a vocalist on the track "Take Off" from the Bob and Doug McKenzie comedy album **The Great White North** (characters that Moranis and Dave Thomas [who, incidentally is the brother of Ian Thomas of "Painted Ladies" fame] portrayed on *SCTV* and in the film *Strange Brew*). "Take Off" was also released as a single in Canada and reached #16 on the US Billboard singles chart, which actually makes it the biggest singles hit that Geddy Lee ever had in the US, as that position was higher than any *Rush* song achieved on the US charts.

Chapter Twenty — Miscellaneous Questions? Answers!

Bibliography

In addition to the thousands of progressive rock albums I own on CD, Vinyl, Cassette, or Digitally, the following printed sources have also been used to help formulate some of the questions.

- *Mojo — The Music Magazine* Issue 73, published December 1999.
- *Classic Rock Magazine* Issue 97, published September 2006.
- *Mojo Classic — Pink Floyd and The Story of Prog Rock*, published circa 2005/2006 (no date is actually published anywhere in the issue, but it includes **Frances the Mute** by *The Mars Volta* as the 18th greatest progressive rock album of all time, an album released in March of 2005. My recollection is that I purchased this magazine not too long after that).
- *Prog Magazine*, Issues 22 (December 2011), 26 (May 2012), 37 (July 2013), 44 (March 2014), 94 (January 2019), and 98 (June 2019).
- *Uncut — Ultimate Music Guide — King Crimson* (Uncut Ultimate Guide Series — 2019, Issue 3).
- Jethro Tull 25th Anniversary Tour and 50th Anniversary Tour programme guides.
- King Crimson Tour Programme — 1995 North American tour.
- Rocking the Classics — English Progressive Rock and the Counterculture, Edward Macan, 1997, Oxford University Press.
- The Music's All That Matters — A History of Progressive Rock, Paul Stump, 1997, Quartet Books Limited.

Bibliography

- *The Progressive Rock Files, 4th Edition,* Jerry Lucky, 1998, Collector's Guide Publishing.

- Listening to the Future — The Time of Progressive Rock, 1968–1978, Bill Martin, 1998, Open Court Publishing.

- Mountains Come Out of the Sky — The Illustrated History of Prog Rock, Will Romano, 2010, Backbeat Books.

- *Beyond and Before — Progressive Rock Since the 1960s,* Paul Hegarty & Martin Halliwell, 2011, Continuum Publishing.

- Prog Rock FAQ — All That's Left to Know About Rock's Most Progressive Music, Will Romano, 2014, Backbeat Books.

- Minstrels in the Gallery — A History of Jethro Tull, David Rees, 1998, Firefly Publishing.

- Flying Colours: The Jethro Tull Reference Manual, Greg Russo, 2000, Crossfire Publishing.

About the Author

Gian-Luca Di Rocco has been a fan of progressive rock for well over 30 years. He liked many of the most famous progressive rock bands for years before he discovered that they were all considered progressive rock bands, not having heard the term before. Once he did, he began to devote more and more of his music collecting and listening to other bands considered squarely or broadly to be in the wider progressive rock music genre. He has never had the time (or perhaps the interest, especially as the number keeps changing all the time) to count the number of progressive rock albums he owns, but estimates it must be upwards of 2000.

This is his fourth book, having previously authored what he believes to be the very first Prog Rock murder mystery novel, *Murder at the Battle of the Bands* (2021), a comedic mystery featuring an all-female nine-member progressive rock band named "The Exquisite Curves." He has also authored two non-fiction books — one on Doctor Who entitled *Identity Lost — A Critical Analysis of the Transformation of the Beloved Television Hero, Dr. Who* (2019), and the other entitled *The Angel Factor — A Critical Appreciation of Charlie's Angels 1976–2019* (2021).

About the Author

Printed in Great Britain
by Amazon